SEW
JELLY ROLL
QUILTS & GIFTS

Dedication

For Rory, Sam and Jack

SEW
JELLY ROLL
QUILTS & GIFTS

CAROLYN FORSTER

First published in Great Britain 2012

Search Press Limited
Wellwood, North Farm Road,
Tunbridge Wells, Kent TN2 3DR

Text copyright © Carolyn Forster 2012

Photographs by Debbie Patterson
Photographs and design copyright
© Search Press Ltd 2012

ISBN: 978-1-84448-754-7

The Publishers and author can accept no responsibility for any consequences arising from the information, advice or instructions given in this publication.

Readers are permitted to reproduce any of the items/patterns in this book for their personal use, or for the purposes of selling for charity, free of charge and without the prior permission of the Publishers. Any use of the items/patterns for commercial purposes is not permitted without the prior permission of the Publishers.

Suppliers
For details of suppliers, please visit the Search Press website: www.searchpress.com.

Some of the Jelly Rolls™ used in this book may no longer be available. Look for something similar or cut fabrics from your stash. Fabric collections come and go very quickly, as do Jelly Rolls™. It is always worth buying a Jelly Roll™ when you find one that inspires you and keeping it until the right project comes along.

Publisher's note
All the step-by-step photographs in this book feature the author, Carolyn Forster. No models have been used.

Acknowledgments

With immense thanks to Katie Sparkes and Debbie Patterson for their professionalism and vision for this book.

And, as always, thanks to Craig and Paul for keeping me focused on things other than patchwork!

Many thanks also to the following for quilting the quilts featured in this book: Chris Farrance at The Quilt Room, Dorking, Surrey (Flower Garden, Sweet Sixteen, Tea Time Treat and Woven Dreams); Susie Green at Duxhurst Quilting, Reigate, Surrey (Autumn Floor and Sunny Days); Mimi Hollenbaugh at Puddleducks, Sevenoaks, Kent (Sewing Spools, Ripples and Ohio Star).

Page 1: Sunny Days, see page 60.
Page 3: Ohio Star, see page 88.
Opposite: A glorious selection of Jelly Rolls™.

CONTENTS

INTRODUCTION

When you embark on making a quilt, you want it to look as good as you possibly can, with all the fabrics used working together in a harmonious, stylish design. This is one area, however, that people often have difficulty with. Over the years, the fabric manufacturing industry has come up with a number of ways to help you with your fabric choices, bringing out numerous, wonderful fabric collections to encourage people to sew their own quilts. Choose your fabrics from one collection and you can rest assured they will all coordinate, because that is the way they were designed.

The next question is how much of each fabric to buy. In the past, the fabrics would have been cut from bolts, 9¾in (0.25m) being the usual minimum. Very few of us had a budget that would allow us to buy this amount of every fabric in a collection, so when the manufacturers started putting together pre-cut bundles of fabrics spanning an entire range at a price we could afford, we had no more excuses – we bought those pre-cuts and got sewing!

Jelly Rolls™, made by the fabric manufacturer Moda, have been one of the most popular pre-cut bundles. Each bundle contains 40 pre-cut 2½in (6.5cm) wide strips of coordinating fabrics, allowing you to start sewing your quilt straight away, with most of the cutting already done for you. To personalise the quilt you can choose your own fabrics to use as a background or border.

In this book I have given you a selection of simple quilts that can be sewn speedily from Jelly Rolls™ and similar products (see pages 8–9). To make life easy, the bindings to finish each quilt use the pre-cut strips too. In addition, to make the best use of your 2½in (6.5cm) wide strips, each quilt is accompanied by a coordinating project, each of which makes an ideal gift or accessory. Every technique is explained clearly, so be inspired, and enjoy making the quilts and gifts in this book using your pre-cut bundles.

WHAT IS A JELLY ROLL?

In the world of patchwork and quilting fabrics, a Jelly Roll™ is the fun name that the fabric company Moda has given to its pre-cut bundle of 2½in (6.5cm) wide fabric strips. The strips are cut across the width of the fabric and are all the same length. The advantage of buying your fabric in the form of Jelly Rolls™ is that it makes the piecing process faster and easier, as nearly all of the cutting and fabric selection has already been done for you.

The name 'Jelly Roll' is derived from the fact that it resembles a jelly roll, also known as a Swiss roll – a rolled-up sponge roll with jam in. Just as indulgent as the cake variety, the fabric kind have fewer calories and last longer, as you can sew them into quilts and gifts that last a lifetime!

Generally, a Jelly Roll™ contains around 40 strips of fabric, each 2½in (6.5cm) wide and approximately 44in (112cm) long. It is a great way to get a piece of every fabric from a particular collection or, if you prefer, you can buy colour-themed or plain Jelly Rolls™. If a fabric collection does not include 40 different designs, there will still be 40 strips in the bundle – it simply means some of the designs will be repeated.

Other manufacturers and shops produce their own rolls, all going by different names but all containing various quantities of pre-cut strips. Check them carefully before you buy these alternative products – all the quilts in this book are based on bundles of 40 strips, so this is the minimum amount you will need.

You can usually find the pre-cut bundles of fabric merchandised alongside the bolts from the same collection, both in shops and on-line. This makes it easy to see what the range of fabric looks like on the bolt, and allows you to buy more for borders, binding and backings as your quilt progresses.

And there is nothing to stop you making your own Jelly Rolls™. Often when I make a quilt, I will cut the fabric I need from the yardage, and then from what is left I cut some 2½in (6.5cm) strips and store these away for when I need them. Alternatively, have fun cutting into your stash so you have a batch of ready-cut strips for when inspiration strikes, or when time is short and you want that quilt sewn-up fast. The instructions for cutting your own strips are provided on pages 14–15.

Note

Jelly Roll™ is the name Moda uses for its 2½in (6.5cm) wide strips, but other companies make their own versions. These go by different names, for example Bali Pops, Design Rolls, Strip-tease Buns, Sushi Rolls, and Roll-ups. They usually contain 40 strips, but check before buying as different manufacturers offer different numbers of strips. All strip widths should be 2½in (6.5cm).

FABRICS & THREADS

FABRICS

The fabrics in a Jelly Roll™ will all coordinate because they are from the same designed fabric collection. However, it may sometimes be necessary to make this selection of fabrics stretch a little further, for example to make a larger quilt, in which case you will probably be looking to add one or two extra fabrics to the mix, in larger quantities and at repeated positions in the quilt's design.

Traditionally, a plain fabric like bleached (white) or unbleached (cream) calico (muslin) was used, and this is still a popular choice today. Take a look at Sweet Sixteen on page 114 or Tea Time Treat on page 98 to see how it works. However, as you can see from some of the other projects, for example Autumn Floor on page 106 and Flower Garden on page 52, I have added other prints that blend well with the collection. In Autumn Floor I added the sashing and the border fabric to go with the pre-selected Jelly Roll™ fabrics, and in Flower Garden I added the background to the flowers, which were sewn from a Jelly Roll™, and then a frame to the blocks. This is a good way to build up confidence with selecting and combining different fabrics. As all

the fabrics in a Jelly Roll™ are pre-selected, it is fun and artistically satisfying to be able to stamp your own identity on a project by adding one or two new fabrics that you have picked yourself.

When you add your own chosen fabrics to the selection, make sure they are a similar weight to the fabrics already used so as not to cause undue strain on the seams or make the project difficult to handle when sewing.

Fat quarters and charm squares

In some of the projects in this book you will come across fat quarters and charm squares. A fat quarter measures approximately 18 x 22in (50 x 56cm). It is a quarter of a square metre of fabric, obtained by cutting 18in (50cm) from the bolt of fabric, and then cutting this in half to give a 'square'. Charm squares are pre-cut fabric squares usually 5 x 5in (13 x 13cm) that include samples from a particular fabric range. They are sold in packs of between 40 and 50 squares. Shops also cut their own; always check the size and selection that you are buying.

SEWING THREADS

I usually choose a pure cotton sewing thread for sewing my quilts, as I am piecing them from cotton fabrics. When sewing such a broad range of different fabrics together, choice of thread colour is very important; you do not want to be continually changing thread as you sew different combinations of fabrics. When selecting your cotton sewing thread, choose a colour that acts as link or a 'shadow' between the colours. For example, if you were sewing a blue and white quilt, I suggest choosing a mid-grey thread, as it is will blend well with both colours.

Other thread colours that you will find useful are cream, dark cream, mid grey, dark grey, black, sludge and tan. Buy each of these colours on as large a spool as you can afford, as this will save you money in the long run. Invest in one spool of each colour and you will find that, for your piecing, there will always be a suitable thread no matter what the combination of fabrics that you are sewing together.

When machine stitching, wind two bobbins before you start sewing. This will allow you to stitch more quickly as you won't have to stop when the bobbin runs out. Just pick up a ready-wound one.

BASIC SEWING EQUIPMENT

SEWING MACHINE

The quilts and projects in this book are speedy because they make use of pre-cut strips of coordinating fabrics and a sewing machine. The only stitch you will need is straight stitch, so there is no need to invest in a fancy machine. Most seam allowances for patchwork are ¼in (0.5cm), so you will need this as a guide on your machine. The easiest way to do this is to fit your machine with a ¼in (0.5cm) piecing foot and use this as your guide. Failing this, you might also want to mark the plate using a piece of masking tape by running a piece of ¼in (0.5cm) graph paper through the machine. Use several layers of masking tape if you want a more definite edge for guiding the fabric against.

In addition to the standard foot that your sewing machine is supplied with, two additional feet will make life easier if you want to machine quilt. A free-motion quilting foot and an even-feed walking foot will help, depending on which sort of quilting you choose to do. The even-feed foot is also very helpful for sewing a binding to your quilt.

OTHER SEWING EQUIPMENT

Scissors

Use a large pair of long-bladed scissors for cutting the fabrics. I have a specialist pair of quilting scissors that is ideal for this purpose. Small scissors with fine points make snipping threads easy and give you more control over the blades.

Quick Unpick

Use this tool to undo sewing mistakes quickly and easily. I also use the point to help guide in the fabric under the machine foot, close to the needle, which helps to protect my fingers.

Pins

Long, fine pins with a glass head are the most useful for keeping fabrics in place before stitching.

Quilter's tape measure

This type of tape measure is longer than normal and so is useful for measuring bed lengths and quilt sides. It is 120in (300cm) long.

Template plastic

This is a sturdy but thin plastic that can be drawn on or traced through and then cut with normal scissors. To write on the plastic, you should use a fine permanent marker pen.

Iron

Your patchwork will need pressing, so a good hot iron is useful. You can use a steam iron, but be careful not to distort the seams when pressing.

Hera marker

This is a useful tool for creasing seams and marking quilting designs.

Chalk marker

This marker is used like a pen and leaves a thin white line on the fabric that brushes off easily. It is ideal for marking on patterns and stitch lines.

Needles for general sewing

Depending on the thread that is used, the needles you work with will vary. Having a selection to hand will give you the most flexibility with your quilting.

Needles for appliqué

I tend to use a small needle for appliqué and, as I hand quilt, I use the same needle to appliqué as I do to quilt. This is a Betweens needle, size 10. If you choose to use appliqué needles, these have a longer eye, which you may find easier to thread.

CUTTING YOUR OWN STRIPS

If you already have a stash of fabrics that you want to use for a Jelly Roll™ project, then there is nothing to stop you cutting your own strips from them. The easiest way to do this is to use a rotary cutter, a cutting mat and a ruler that is 2½in (6.5cm) wide. This makes the measurement you want easy to see, and ensures quick and accurate cutting. Of course, you can use whatever width of ruler you have to hand, in which case you might find it helpful to mark the line that you will most frequently be using with some tape to draw your eye to it easily.

Follow the steps below to ensure neat and accurate cutting. Note that these instructions assume that you are right handed and work from left to right; if you are left handed, work from right to left.

Begin by pre-washing, drying and ironing the fabric. Hold it up with the two selvedges together and make sure the fabric is not twisted. If it is, move the fabric to straighten it out. This may mean that the cut edges are now not even, but these will be trimmed off in any case.

> *Note*
>
> Most fabrics that are designed for patchwork are sold in widths of 42–44in (106–112cm). This is useful to remember if you are buying fabric especially for this purpose.

CUTTING EQUIPMENT

Rulers

Various specialist acrylic rulers are available that work with a rotary cutter and self-healing cutting mat to cut the fabric easily and quickly in layers where necessary. The various types that you could use for the projects in this book are described with the relevant project instructions.

Rotary cutter

Like a pizza wheel, a rotary cutter cuts through up to about eight layers of fabric at a time. Keep the blade sharp and free of nicks, and cut through as many or as few layers as you are comfortable with.

Self-healing cutting mat

This is a purpose-made mat, available from craft stores, on which to cut your fabric using the rulers and cutters. It is marked into a grid that you can use to help you measure and cut the fabric in straight lines. Buy the largest size you can afford, as the larger the cutting mat, the less you will need to fold your fabric.

A selection of rulers, a rotary cutter and cutting mat.

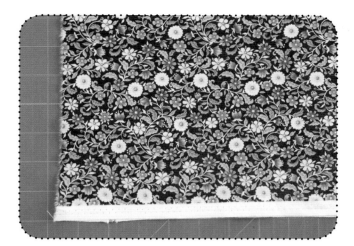

1 Fold your fabric in half as accurately as possible, wrong sides facing and with the selvedges together, and lay it on the cutting mat. Place the fabric with the selvedges at the bottom and aligned with a horizontal line on the background grid.

2 Use the ruler and cutter to trim off the raw edge on the left-hand side: align the ruler with a vertical line on the grid and trim off a straight edge approximately ¾in (2cm) in from the side. Hold the ruler in place and push the cutter away from you, starting at the selvedge. Keep the cutter firmly against the ruler while cutting to ensure a straight and even edge.

3 Lift off the ruler and remove the fabric. Replace the ruler so that it lies 2½in (6.5cm) from the edge and cut your first strip.

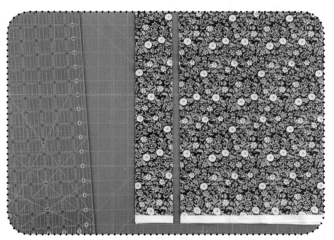

4 Remove the ruler and put the fabric strip to one side. Replace the ruler and continue, cutting as many strips as you need.

Note

You can pile up to eight layers of fabric together for cutting, but you will need a sharp blade and a firm hand. Work with as many or as few layers as you are comfortable with.

HOW MANY SHAPES PER STRIP?

For reference, it is helpful when working on your own projects to know how many shapes you can expect to cut from a strip.

One 42in (106.5cm) strip yields:
Sixteen 2½in (6.5cm) squares
Nine 2½ x 4½in (6.5 x 11.5cm) rectangles
Four 2½ x 8½in (6.5 x 21.5cm) rectangles
Twenty-four half-square triangles
Twelve quarter-square triangles

CUTTING SQUARES AND RECTANGLES

1 Lay the folded strip of fabric horizontally on the cutting mat, aligned with the background grid with the selvedge on the left-hand side, and cut off the selvedge.

2 Discard the selvedge and measure along with the ruler to where you want to cut – 2½in (6.5cm) for a square; 4½in (11.5cm) or 8½in (21.5cm) for a rectangle. Align the ruler with the grid and cut. Lift up the ruler, remove the shape, and continue to cut more shapes like this as you need them.

CUTTING TRIANGLES

Not every shape you need will be a square or a rectangle. For triangles, because of the added complication of accommodating the seam allowance, it is best to use specialist rulers. These are available for cutting half-square triangles (squares cut into two triangles) or quarter-square triangles (squares cut into four triangles). Follow the manufacturer's instructions as to ruler placement, as they all vary slightly. Some companies have made templates to fit the 2½in (6.5cm) strips that enable you to cut hexagons, kites and coneheads.

On the opposite page I have demonstrated how to use two types of specialist ruler for cutting triangles. The first type is a right-angled triangle ruler designed to be used with the horizontal and vertical sides aligned with the grain of the fabric. The diagonal edge includes a ¼in (0.5cm) seam allowance. The second type is a quarter-square triangle ruler, where the longest edge of the triangle is cut on the straight of the grain.

Vertical and horizontal sides aligned with grain of fabric

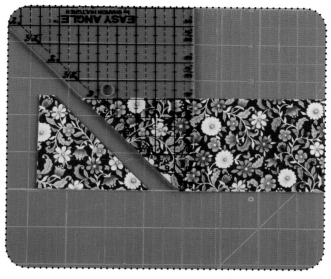

1 Place the folded fabric strip on the cutting mat and align it with the grid. Place the triangular ruler on the fabric, aligning the short horizontal edge of the ruler with the top of the fabric and the long vertical edge with the left-hand edge. Cut off the triangle along the diagonal edge of the ruler.

2 Remove the cut triangle and replace the ruler, this time turned through 180° with the diagonal side aligned with the diagonally cut edge of the fabric. Cut your next triangle.

Longest side aligned with grain of fabric

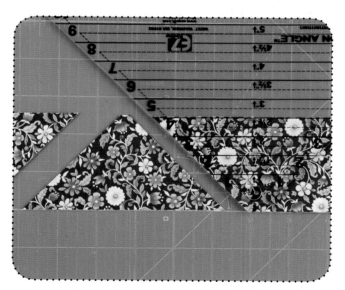

1 Place the folded fabric strip on the cutting mat and align it with the grid, as before. Place the triangular ruler on the fabric, aligning one of the marked lines with the grain of the fabric. Cut off the left-hand triangle along the left-hand edge of the ruler, then continue holding the ruler in place and cut along the right-hand edge of the triangle, as shown.

2 Remove the fabric triangle and reposition the triangle, this time turned through 180° with the point at the bottom, and cut along the right-hand edge.

STITCHING THE PATCHWORK

Finger pressing.

Here are some hints and tips to help you when stitching your patchwork on the sewing machine.

Before you begin

Read through all the instructions before you start on a project. Make sure you have all the materials and equipment you need, and that you are familiar with the techniques used. For the projects in this book:

- all seam allowances are ¼in (0.5cm) unless otherwise stated
- all fabric cut off the bolt is cut across the width, including your Jelly Roll™ strips if you are cutting these yourself (see page 14), unless otherwise stated
- all fabric quantities are based on a 42in (106.5cm) useable width of fabric.

Threading the needle

When threading the needle, I always find it easier to hold the thread and put the needle over the thread, rather than trying to poke a piece of thread through the needle's eye. If you find threading the needle difficult, then invest in a needle threader. For pulling the needle through the layers when using some of the bulkier threads, use a 'grabber' to help.

Stitch length

When machine stitching, set your straight-stitch length to 11 or 2.0 to 2.5, depending on how your machine is calibrated. It needs to be small enough to hold the fabrics together, but large enough to unpick easily, if the need arises.

When you are sewing fabric strips together that will then be cut and re-sewn (see page 20), you may want to set the stitch length a little smaller than usual so that the stitches do not come undone easily when they are cut through.

Pressing

This is done with a hot iron and a pressing pad or ironing board. Whether you use steam or not is up to you; some people think it distorts the work, but this hasn't been my experience.

I do press my work from the front and not from the back. I find that by doing this I eliminate the little pleats that often occur when you press from the back, which then have to be removed by pressing from the front, so the process takes twice as long!

Take care to position the work and the seam you want to press correctly; you will then find you can press in one stroke.

Finger pressing

Finger pressing (shown above) involves squeezing the fabric between your fingers and is a quick method of marking the fabric. It leaves a semi-permanent crease and is a more accurate way of marking than pinning. It also eliminates the need to put a pin in that will then immediately need to be removed.

CHAIN PIECING

This method of joining fabric pieces involves continuously feeding the fabric pieces in under the machine foot, one after the other, with a gap of about ½in (1cm) between them. The pieces are held together by the sewing thread, hence the term 'chain piecing'. The advantage of this method is that it saves on thread when you have to sew lots of patches together in pairs.

1 Lay two fabric pieces together, right sides facing, and stitch along the seam. When you reach the end, position the next pair of fabric pieces ready for stitching, leaving a gap of about ½in (1cm). Stitch across the gap and then along the next seam.

2 When you have stitched all the fabric pieces, simply snip through the threads joining them together.

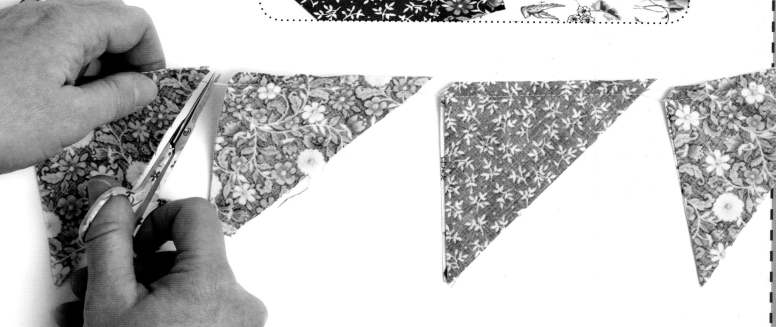

SEW-AND-CUT TECHNIQUE

Usually, when sewing a patchwork, you will cut out lots of the shapes that you need individually and then sew them together. Sometimes, however, it is quicker and more accurate to sew a set of strips of fabric together first and then cut them into units. This method is useful when your design includes blocks made from squares or rectangles, as on the Sweet Sixteen and Autumn Floor quilts, or when the design is made up of lots of long strips, for example Ohio Star.

Here I will show you how to sew a nine-patch block. It is a square made from nine patches of fabric. Instead of cutting out nine separate little squares then sewing them together, you can stitch strips together in rows then cut them up and re-sew to create the block.

Note

Starting to stitch from alternate ends of the fabric (see step 2 below) prevents the fabric from stretching in one direction and distorting.

1 Lay two strips together, right sides facing, and align the raw edges. Stitch down one side.

2 Fold open the strips and lay a third strip on top of the second, right sides facing. Stitch down the seam, starting from the end you have just finished at.

3 Press the fabric on the front, ensuring all the seams are pressed in the same direction.

4 Cut off the selvedge, following the method on page 16, step 1.

5 Cut the fabric into strips. Here, they are 2½in (6.5cm) wide.

6 Repeat steps 1–5 with a different set of fabrics, if desired, as I did for the block shown. Lay two patchwork strips together, right sides facing. Ensure the seams are aligned, and are pressed in opposite directions.

7 Place the fabric under the needle with the seams facing in the direction of sewing. Sew the strips together, guiding the seams under the needle as you stitch.

8 Fold open the patchwork and place the third strip on top of the second, right sides facing. Stitch the strips together as before.

Note

Always place the largest piece on the bottom and the strip you are adding on the top.

9 Press the seams flat by ironing on the front of the fabric.

The finished block.

APPLIQUÉ

Appliqué essentially means stitching fabrics down on top of each other. The stitch I use to do this is known as appliqué stitch and I use the same stitch to secure the bindings on the back of a quilt (see pages 36–39). Use a sewing thread to match the fabric you are stitching down, and cut a length of thread as long as your arm for ease of stitching. If you are using a template, freezer paper is ideal as, when ironed, the shiny side sticks to the fabric. This stabilises the fabric while you work with it.

1 Cut a template from freezer paper and iron it, shiny side down, on to the wrong side of the fabric. The heat will cause the template to stick to the fabric.

2 Cut around the template, leaving a ¼in (0.5cm) seam allowance.

3 Turn the seam over and tack it in place, going through all the layers of fabric and the template.

4 Pin the shape in position on the patchwork. Insert the needle to come up from the back of the work, hiding the knot. Bring the needle up through the edge of the fold of the top piece of fabric and pull the thread through.

5 Take the needle back down through the background fabric only, in the same position as it came up, making a tiny stitch over the edge of the top piece of fabric.

6 Take the needle about ⅛in (0.25cm) along the back of the work and then bring it back through the folded edge of the fabric. Repeat this, creating a row of tiny stitches on the front of the work and longer, slanted stitches on the back. Leave a 1in (2.5cm) gap.

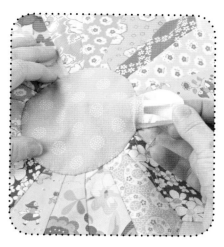

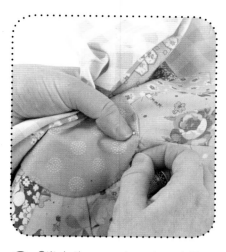

7 Remove the tacking stitches.

8 Remove the paper template by pulling it through the gap in the stitching. Use your fingers or a pair of tweezers, whichever is easier.

9 Stitch the opening closed. To fasten off, leave the needle on the back of the work and stitch two or thee stitches on top of each other through the background fabric only in an area hidden behind the appliqué work.

ADDING BORDERS/FRAMES

When adding borders or frames to your patchwork, it is best to pin them in place first to ensure all the parts fit together. Start by folding the strip of fabric into halves and then quarters. Mark these points either with a pin or by finger pressing. Do the same with the side of the block or quilt that the strip will be sewn on to.

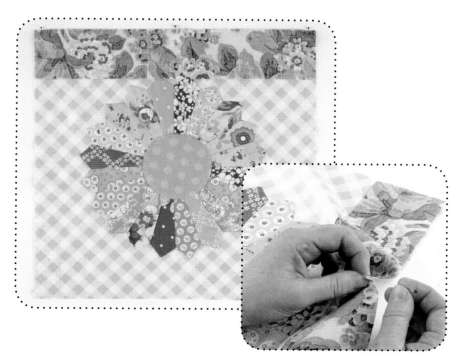

Next, match up the start and finish of the strip with the beginning and end of the block or quilt side, and then the quarter- and halfway marks. Pin the strip in place, right sides facing. When you start to stitch, remove the pins as you come to them.

BASIC QUILTING MATERIALS

Once you have sewn your patchwork top, it is ready for layering with wadding (also known as batting) and backing fabric, and then quilting.

BACKING FABRIC

Choose a fabric that is a similar weight to that used on the front of the quilt. If you are hand quilting you will want a fabric that will be easy to work with, whereas if you decide to machine quilt, you can get away with a slightly heavier-weight fabric, as the machine will be doing the hard work, not your fingers.

The backing can be a patterned or plain fabric. If you choose plain, remember that your quilting stitches will be highly visible, whereas a patterned fabric will hide them.

The backing fabric will need to be wider and longer than the patchwork top in order to accommodate the shrinkage or 'pulling up' of the top and the wadding when you quilt. The surplus fabric (and wadding) can be trimmed off when you come to bind the quilt.

A contrasting floral backing fabric works well with the strong geometric design on the front of this quilt. This quilt is called Tea Time Treat and the instructions for making it begin on page 98.

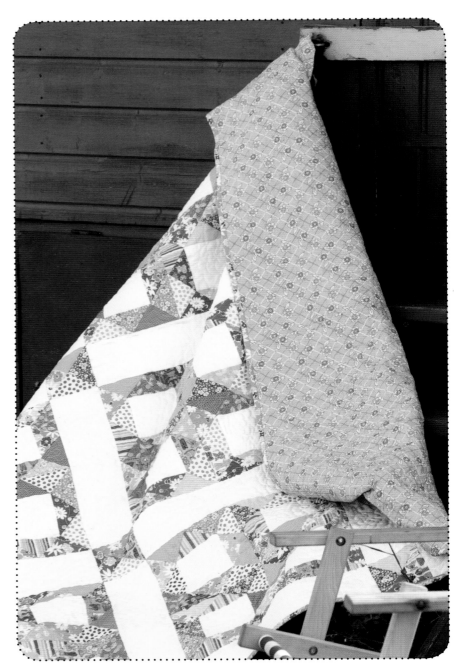

Joining the backing fabric

To avoid seams on the back of the quilt, use wide-width fabrics. If, however, you do choose a fabric that needs joining, follow these basic instructions:

Remove the selvedges from the sides of the fabric. Sew the seam using a ¼in (0.5cm) seam allowance and press the seam open. This will reduce the bulky areas you need to quilt through. Seams can be horizontal or vertical (diagrams a and b), or you can cut the second width of fabric in half lengthways (diagram c) and join each half to either side of the full width. This method ensures the seams do not come under so much stress when the quilt is folded.

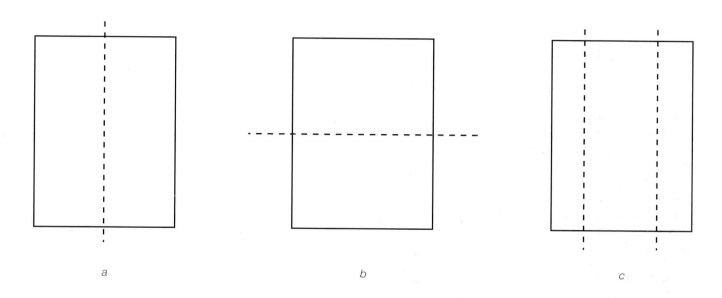

a   b   c

WADDING

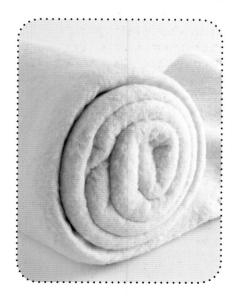

Wadding (also known as batting) is the soft filling that goes between the patchwork top and the backing fabric. It can be made from polyester, cotton (or a combination of both), wool, and even recycled plastic bottles or sustainably grown bamboo. The important things to think about are how much quilting you want to do and how 'puffy' you want the quilt to be. This 'puffiness' is called 'loft' and it gives the quilt its characteristic look.

All wadding/batting states on the packaging how far apart you can space the quilting. If you do not want to do too much quilting, then one that recommends quilting up to 10in (25.5cm) apart would be a good choice. For more quilting, choose a wadding that needs quilting every 2–4in (5–10cm). Ask other quilters what they use, and they might give you an off-cut that you can try out before buying.

HOOP

A quilting hoop will help keep your work flat as you quilt. Some people quilt without one, but generally for a large quilt it will make the quilting easier. Choose a size that you can handle easily; 14in (35.5cm) is a good size.

QUILTING THREAD

Quilting thread is slightly thicker than general sewing thread and forms the quilting stitches that hold the three layers of a quilt together. The reels that you buy will state whether they are for hand or machine quilting (sometimes they will work well for both).

Choose a colour that blends with the overall appearance of the quilt, unless you want the stitches to stand out on particular areas. Remember that for hand quilting, the thread will be visible as small stitches, but for machine quilting you will see a continuous line of thread on the front and back of the quilt.

QUILTING NEEDLES

Also known as Betweens, these are usually short needles with a round eye. They are available in a range of sizes to accommodate different threads and skill levels. If you are a beginner I suggest you start with a size 8 and aim to work up to using a 10 or 11, which are smaller. Generally, the smaller the needle the smaller the stitch you make, but this also depends on experience and the particular combination of fabrics and wadding you are using. As a rule, use the needle size that is most comfortable in your hand.

For machine quilting you will usually need to change the needle in your sewing machine from a general sewing needle to a 'jeans' or machine quilting needle. Practice and knowledge of your machine will help you work out which is the best one to use.

TACKING THREAD

Use a specialist tacking/basting thread for hand tacking, as it can be broken easily and is cheaper than regular sewing thread, but holds the layers together securely for quilting.

THIMBLES

Thimbles help protect your fingers during the quilting process. I wear a round-topped, dimpled thimble on the middle finger of my right hand (shown on the right in the picture above) to help push the needle through the quilt. On my left hand, which is under the quilt, I wear a flat-topped thimble with a ridge on my index finger (shown on the left). The ridge helps me to create the quilting stitch as it pushes the fabric up. Make sure your thimbles fit comfortably. It may take a little time to get used to wearing them, but persevere as it will prevent your fingers from getting very sore.

LAYERING & BASTING

In this section I will explain how to assemble the layers and hold them together ready for quilting. This is also known as basting. Generally, for all methods of basting (except spray glue), the securing method should form a grid pattern, often dictated by the patches in the quilt. There should usually be no gaps bigger than 6–8in (15–20.5cm) between the basting, which is approximately the size of your spread hand. If the patchwork does not have a grid to follow, use your hand span as a ready guide.

LAYERING

Work on a flat floor that is already clear and where the quilt can be laid out flat. This saves you having to move your furniture around to make room for the quilt on the floor. Community and church halls often have a suitable space – make sure you book it when you know the cleaner has just been, and consider using a kneeling mat or knee pads to protect your knees. Alternatively, they might have a large table that you could use. A carpeted floor will stop the quilt moving so much and the edges can be secured with masking tape.

You might also consider using the services of a long-arm quilter. Many offer a basting service, which leaves you free to sit down and simply enjoy the quilting.

1 Press the backing fabric and lay it on the floor, wrong side up. Pat it flat gently. Secure it to the floor with tabs of masking tape at the corners and at the mid points on all four sides. Do not stretch the fabric, as this will result in puckering once the basting is complete and the masking tape removed.

2 Lay the wadding/batting on top of the backing fabric. If it helps, fold the wadding into four, line up the wadding with a corner of the backing fabric and unfold it a quarter at a time. This way, the middle of the backing and the wadding are aligned and you don't need to spend time re-adjusting to line the materials up. Pat the wadding flat.

3 Press the patchwork top for the last time and place it on top of the wadding, right side up. Again, fold it into quarters if this helps. Remember to leave a margin around the outside edge of the wadding. Pat flat. Add some tabs of masking tape at the corners.

Your quilt is now ready for basting.

HAND BASTING

Hand basting a quilt gives you the best control over the layers of the quilt and does not add any extra weight or bulk. Start with a backstitch and a knot and work the stitches from right to left (left to right if you are left handed). The stitches should be about ½in (1cm) long and evenly spaced. Finish with a backstitch to keep the thread secure. Use a long, strong needle to work in and out of the layers with the tacking thread. Popular choices are Cotton Darners or Sharps size 8.

When basting a quilt I find it easier to work to a standard grid system. If I always use the same system, then I don't have to think or plan, just baste!

1 Pin the three layers together in the centre, at the corners and the mid point on each side. This is to keep everything in place while you baste.

2 With the tacking thread, start with a knot and a backstitch and baste the diagonals. Finish with a backstitch (diagram a).

3 Now baste across the middle in both directions (diagram b). As you come across the pins, take them out.

4 Using your hand span as a guide, baste in rows from the centre towards the outside edge. When this section is full, move round to the next section. There are four sections to fill in this way, always starting from the middle and working towards the outside edge (diagrams c to f).

5 When complete, baste ¼in (0.5cm) away from the outside edge of the quilt sandwich. This will be removed as the quilt gradually shifts when you quilt it, but in the meantime it will stop the edges from becoming tatty or stretched.

> **Note**
>
> You should never need to have your hand under the quilt; you are working from the top all time. In this way, you do not disturb the layers.

a

b

c

d

e

f

> **Note**
>
> To help ease the needle up through the layers use a teaspoon or a grapefruit spoon. As the needle and your hands are always on the top of the quilt, your fingers can get sore as the needle pushes up against them, so by pushing the needle up against the edge of a teaspoon or grapefruit spoon the process will become quicker.

6 Remove the masking tape and pick the quilt (and yourself) up from the floor.

7 If you like, you can now fold over the extra wadding and backing fabric and tack along the edge of the quilt.

SAFETY-PIN BASTING

This basting method involves using 1in (2.5cm) safety pins that have coloured plastic covers for ease of use.

1 Lay out the quilt sandwich (see page 27), but do not pin.

2 Starting from the centre of the quilt, use the safety pins to hold the layers together. The pins should be neither too dense nor too sparse. If you can spread your hand out on the quilt and touch pins at the tip of your little finger and thumb, that is a good density.

3 Working from the middle of the quilt, insert a pin and bring it back up through all three layers. Use a teaspoon or a grapefruit spoon to ease your fingers as you manipulate the pin and clip it closed.

4 When the quilt is covered with pins, tack around the edge as explained above.

Safety-pin basting.

Some people find it easier on the hands to use the safety pins with pin covers. These make the pins easier to grip. Also, the open pins do not stick together in clumps when stored, so it is quick and easy to pull out one pin at a time. The Kwik Klip® is a special tool designed for closing the pins easily.

USING SPRAY GLUE

Spray glues, such as 505, offer a convenient way to keep the layers together while you quilt. Use in a ventilated space, and protect surfaces with paper before you start. Follow the manufacturer's instructions, spraying the glue 6in (15cm) above the surface and not over-gluing.

QUILTING

Before you start to quilt, make sure you know how to start and stop stitching securely. This will avoid you wasting time going back over stitches that have come undone.

The length of thread you work with should be as long as your arm. This may not seem very long, but the thread is less likely to become tangled and knot than a longer thread. It will also make the stitching process itself easier: it is a more comfortable stretch of the arm when stitching, and instead of having to pull a long thread skywards you will be pivoting from the elbow, which is a lot less tiring.

SETTING THE QUILT IN A HOOP

Many people prefer to quilt using a hoop. Remember, when putting the quilt in the hoop, that you do not want it tight. The hoop keeps the layers flat, and you need to retain enough flexibility in the quilt to be able to move the needle up and down comfortably.

STARTING TO STITCH

First, tie a knot in the end of the thread you have just cut, then thread the other end into a needle. I find it easier to put the needle over the thread rather than poke the thread into the hole of the needle.

Setting the quilt in a hoop.

1 Insert the needle through the top layer of fabric and wadding to come up where you want to start stitching.

2 Pull the thread through so that the knot is embedded in the wadding. The embedded thread will be quilted over, adding an extra layer of security for the stitching.

Note

What if the knot won't pull through the fabric? If the knot is stubborn, use the point of the needle to gently expand the hole in the fabric that the knot needs to go through. Gently pull the thread until the knot goes into the wadding and then use the needle to push the fabric threads back in place.

FINISHING OFF

When you need to stop stitching or the thread is running out, you will need to finish off securely. To do this, make sure you leave about 5–6in (13–15cm) of thread.

1 Make the last stitch and take the needle all the way through to the back of the quilt.

2 Bring the needle back up at the beginning of the stitch.

3 Pull the thread through and wrap it around the needle three times, keeping the thread close to the quilt, as shown.

4 Take the needle back through the fabric and into the wadding, just underneath the middle of the last stitch.

5 Take the needle through the wadding and bring it up a needle's length away from the stitch. As you pull the thread, a knot will form.

6 Pull the knot through gently to embed it in the wadding. Finish by snipping the tail thread close to the top fabric.

LITTLE-STITCH QUILTING

Little-stitch or fine-hand quilting is a simple running stitch that holds the three layers of a quilt together and creates a textured design all over the quilt. Historically, it was considered important to make your stitches as small as possible, perhaps up to fourteen to the inch. Today, the fashion is for larger stitches, but it is important that you develop a rhythm or evenness to your stitching. In contrast, big-stitch quilting uses a thicker thread and a bigger needle than those suggested on page 26. Choose which style you are comfortable with and which suits your quilt better.

In the picture below, little-stitch quilting is shown on the left and big-stitch quilting on the right.

BIG-STITCH QUILTING

Big-stitch style of hand quilting uses a thicker thread and bigger stitches than the finer little-stitch quilting. The stitch length is often longer on the top surface of the quilt than on the bottom. The designs are usually more widely spaced, therefore it quilts up faster and gives the quilt a bolder, chunkier, more primitive feel. It is sometimes referred to as depression stitch or naïve quilting.

The needle you use should be a Chenille size 22 or 24, Betweens size 3 or 5, or a Sashiko needle. These needles all have a relatively large eye and thick shaft, to pull the thicker thread through easily. A pearl cotton size 8 or 12 is a good choice of thread for big-stitch quilting.

As you make the stitches, try to work with a rhythm to create large, even stitches that go through all three layers. Some people keep the hand that is holding the needle still and move the fingers that are on the underside of the quilt to create the stitches, while others do the opposite. Try different motions to see which is comfortable for you and creates the even stitches you want.

I find it helpful to have a thimble on the middle finger of the needle hand for pushing the needle through, and a ridged thimble on the index finger of the hand under the quilt (see page 26). This finger pushes the layers up, creating a little hill with the ridge of the thimble, which the needle is pushed against, making the stitch.

Big-stitch quilting in bright, contrasting colours (shown below) creates a bold statement.

MACHINE QUILTING

The running stitch that holds the three layers together can be stitched on the sewing machine. To make it easier to work, the quilt will need to be on a table that supports both the machine and the quilt without the quilt dragging. Generally, the machine will need to be fitted with a quilting or 'jeans' needle and a specialist machine-quilting thread should be used (see page 26). Your usual supplier will be able to advise you on what to select, and it is always good to try different makes of thread to see which works best for you.

The open-toe darning foot is used for free-motion quilting.

Free-motion quilting

This method of quilting on the machine allows you to move the stitches in any direction over the quilt and to make the stitches any length. This will usually involve dropping the feed dogs and using an open-toe darning foot, but check the manual for your particular sewing machine. Designs that would be worked in this way include the vermicelli quilting on the Woven Dreams quilt (see below and page 44).

Straight-line quilting

For this method of machine quilting, the stitch length is set by you on the machine. You may find it easier to use an even-feed (walking) foot as it helps all the layers work through at the same pace and prevents dragging. This foot can also be used when you bind the quilt for the same reason. The cross-hatch quilting on the Flower Garden quilt (shown below and on page 52) is an example of this.

The even-feed (walking) foot is used for straight-line quilting and binding.

(Below) Section of the Woven Dreams quilt showing vermicelli quilting.

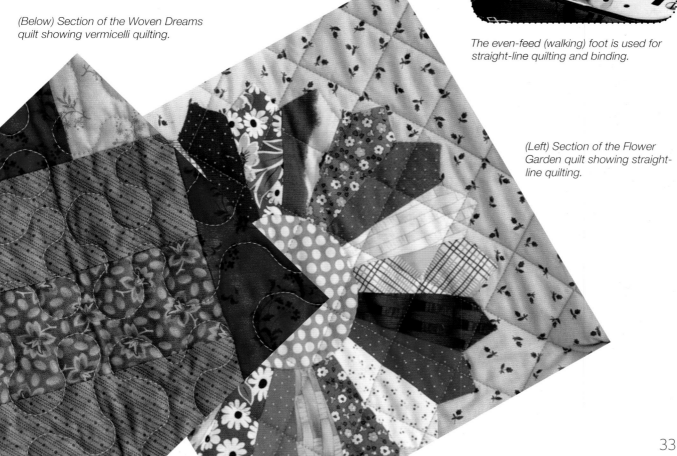

(Left) Section of the Flower Garden quilt showing straight-line quilting.

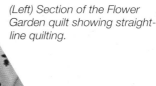

QUILTING DESIGNS

The projects in this book have been machine quilted in a selection of designs, but the ones that are most suitable for your own quilts are vermicelli, Amish wave, cross-hatch quilting and outline quilting. Vermicelli is better suited to machine quilting whereas Amish wave is more appropriate if you are quilting by hand. Cross-hatch quilting and outline quilting work equally well whether you are machine or hand quilting.

Outline quilting

This is where the quilting stitch is worked around the shapes, usually ¼in (0.5cm) away from the seam (shown right).

Cross-hatch quilting

The design can be worked over the entire top of the quilt. Use a long acrylic ruler and Hera marker for marking the lines, either using the patchwork design to help you position the lines or drawing on your own lines over the patchwork. The lines should lie at 45° across the quilt, though an alternative to this is to angle the lines at 60°. You can also stitch horizontal lines across the points of the diamonds to create triangles. All of these options are shown in the diagrams below.

Example of outline quilting using big-stitch quilting.

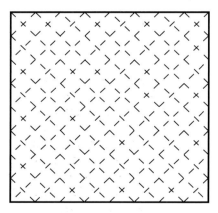

Diagonal lines placed at 45° angles.

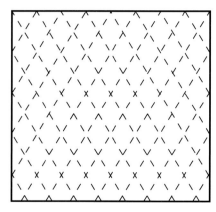

Diagonal lines placed at 60° angles.

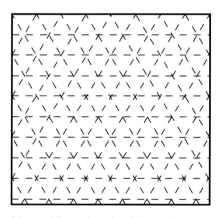

Diagonal lines placed at 60° angles with horizontal lines creating equilateral triangles.

Vermicelli quilting

This is an all-over quilting design that can be worked by machine over any patchwork pattern. The free-motion design is worked on the machine with the feed dogs lowered and an open-toe darning foot in place. The pattern is self-guided and you can control the density of stitching yourself.

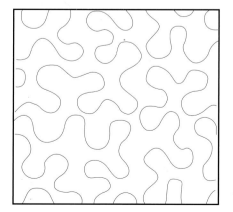

Vermicelli quilting.

Amish wave

This is a fan-shaped design that is quilted either from the outside edge of the quilt in towards the centre, or in rows from bottom to top. In the example at the bottom of the page I have worked the design in rows. It is easy to execute, and many individuals and church groups have used it over the years. For this reason, the basic fan-shaped design goes by various names, each associated with a particular group that used it frequently, for example Amish wave, Mennonite fan, Baptist fan, and simply Wave. A template for the Amish wave design is provided on page 125.

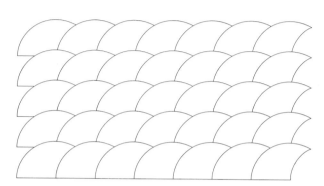

Amish wave worked in rows from the bottom to the top.

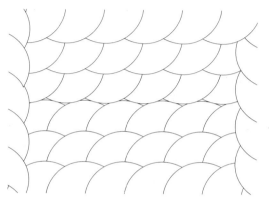

Amish wave worked from the outside in.

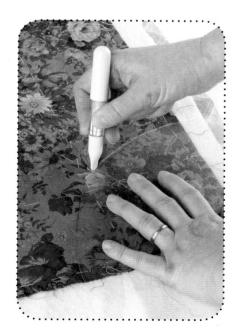

1 Place the template in the bottom right-hand corner of the quilt (the left-hand corner if you are left handed). Draw around the arc.

2 Move the template along, aligning the right-hand edge of the template with the left-hand edge of the first arc, and draw the second shape. Continue in this way along the base of the fabric.

3 The marked arcs are then quilted, top to bottom. Depending on the accuracy of the quilter, these large arcs can contain varying numbers of smaller arcs. These inner arcs can be quilted by eye or marked with a dashed line and then quilted. The distance between the curves is usually measured using either the length of the needle or the width of your thumb knuckle.

BINDING

Once the quilt is quilted, remove any tacking/basting stitches or pins. The quilt is now ready for binding. Here I will show you two ways to bind your quilt: with either square corners or mitred corners. First, you need to join the fabric strips together to make a continuous length that goes all the way around your quilt.

JOINING STRIPS TOGETHER

I use a bias join for joining strips together, which means there is less bulk when the fabric is folded over and wrapped around the edge of the quilt.

1 Take a fabric strip and lay a second fabric strip at 90° on top of it, right sides facing. Allow an extra ½in (1cm) of fabric along each short edge. Stitch across the diagonal.

2 Join subsequent strips using chain piecing (see page 19). Open out the first two strips and lay a third strip face down on the end of the second strip, as in step 1. Stitch across the diagonal. Continue to add fabric strips until you have a piece that is long enough to go all round the quilt.

3 Trim off the excess fabric at each join, leaving a ¼in (0.5cm) seam allowance, and cut through the joining threads. Press all the seams open neatly.

Mock bias join

This type of join is used in continuous mitred binding.

1 Fold in the end of the strip at 90°, and fold and press the whole strip in half, wrong sides together.

2 Trim off the excess fabric at the end of the strip, leaving a ¼in (0.5cm) seam allowance.

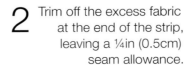

CONTINUOUS MITRED BINDING

This type of binding has a mock bias join to complete the two ends.
Start by fitting an even-feed (walking) foot to your sewing machine.

1 Lay the binding along one side of the quilt, raw edges aligned and starting about one-third of the way along. Pin it in place. I do not usually trim the wadding and backing to match the quilt front until the first steps of the binding are complete, but if you want to trim them now, you can do so.

2 Using the width of the even-feed (walking) foot to gauge the binding width, start stitching about 4in (10cm) away from the end of the binding. Sew down towards the corner, stopping ¼in (0.5cm) away from the edge. Secure the stitches.

3 Remove the quilt from under the machine and fold the binding at 90° away from the quilt so that it lies in a straight line, aligned with the next raw edge.

4 Fold the binding back down on to the quilt, aligning the raw edges and creating a fold at the corner.

5 Start sewing at the folded edge and secure the stitches. Sew down to the next corner and repeat. Turn all the corners in the same way.

6 When you get to the last side, stitch towards the join and stop about 6in (15cm) away from it. Trim the binding at an angle so that it overlaps the start by ½in (1cm).

7 Tuck the end into the start of the binding, as shown.

8 Continue stitching along the binding to secure the two ends. Stitch the join by hand.

9 Remove the quilt from the sewing machine. Trim away the wadding and backing fabric, if you haven't already done so.

10 Turn the binding over to the back of the quilt and pin it in place so that the folded edge meets up with the machine-stitched line.

11 When all the sides are pinned, fold the corners so that the bulk of the fabric lies under the fold and pin them in place.

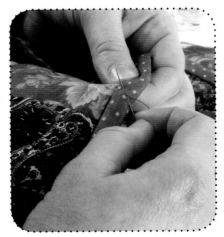

12 Using appliqué stitch (see page 22) and a thread to match the binding, sew the binding to the backing fabric. Do not sew through to the front of the quilt, and hide the travelling stitches in the wadding. When you reach a join, stitch along it.

13 Stitch the join round to the front of the fabric, then take the needle through to the back of the quilt and continue along.

14 As you reach each of the mitred corners, stitch them closed.

SQUARE-CORNERED BINDING

This is a simple basic binding to use when you want to add some colour and strength to the edge of your quilt. You can use a different fabric on each side, and it is a good way of using up odd Jelly Roll™ strips as you cut the fabric 2½in (6.5cm) wide. This version is sewn on the machine and finished by hand. This type of binding is used to edge the coasters on pages 102–105.

Begin by cutting strips of binding 2½in (6.5cm) wide and join them with a crossway join so that you have four strips about 2in (5cm) longer than each side of the quilt. Press them in half lengthways, wrong sides together.

1 Sew one strip to the side of the quilt, matching the raw edges and using the width of the presser foot as your seam allowance. When you reach the end, trim the binding to line up with the top fabric if necessary. Repeat this process on the opposite side of the quilt.

2 Trim off the surplus backing and wadding in line with the raw edge of the binding. Finger press the binding away from the quilt top.

3 Repeat on the remaining sides of the quilt, aligning the raw edges of each strip with the raw edges of the binding strips already attached.

4 At the corners, trim away the surplus fabric and wadding to make turning the binding in easier.

5 Fold the binding over on to the back of the quilt and pin it in place. Fold the corners so that the raw edges are concealed. Slipstitch the folded edge down, sewing along the open edges at the corners (see appliqué stitch on page 22).

LABELLING & LAUNDERING

Once your quilt is sewn and bound it is worth giving a thought to labelling it. Quilts are designed to last a very long time, and a label bearing your name and the date will serve as an enduring reminder of your quilt's origins. If it is for a gift, you can add a short message and perhaps the recipient's name too.

BASIC LABELS

The labelling can be written directly on to the back of the quilt with a permanent marker pen or on to a calico (muslin) label that is then stitched to the quilt.

Pre-printed labels

Many craft shops sell fabrics consisting of decorative blank labels. Buy these by the metre to cut out and use on your projects. Labels can also be ordered from name-tape suppliers, and you can customise these with various motifs and phrases.

Embroidered and cross-stitched labels

Many talented quilters embroider too. Consider embellishing your written label with simple stitching such as backstitch. With a little planning and some graph paper, you can work a cross-stitch label. A special canvas, known as waste canvas, can be used on top of the calico and the threads pulled away afterwards to leave your stitching on the calico.

Printed computer labels

If writing your label is proving a little daunting, then you can produce one on the computer instead. Simply create your label as a document and then print it out on to special fabric sheets. Just follow the instructions to make the printing permanent, and stitch the label to the quilt.

LAUNDERING QUILTS

Once your quilt is finished it may need laundering. This will freshen the quilt after so much handling and remove any markings that were made during the quilting. Also, depending on the wadding used, laundering will shrink the quilt a little and emphasise the quilting stitches.

Quilts are quite sturdy and can easily be washed in a washing machine. Only antique and fragile quilts are best washed by hand.

I put my quilts in the machine on a gentle cycle at 40°C with detergent specially formulated for colours. If you are concerned about colour bleeding, put in a few 'colour catchers'.

On a windy day I will dry the quilt on a clothes line outside. If I cannot do that then I will put it in the tumble dryer long enough to take out the excess water, then I put it in the airing cupboard or over a clothes airer. Once the quilt is dry it can be used straight away – it will not need ironing.

QUILT SIZE

'Will this quilt fit my bed?' is one of the most common questions I am asked. Unfortunately, there is no short answer to this, just a lot more questions!

For example, do you want a quilt that reaches the floor on two sides, three sides or not at all? Does your bedstead have an end? Do you want the quilt to come up and over the pillow? If so, do you want to allow for a tuck under the pillow?

Everyone will want something slightly different so to make sure your quilt is the right size, it is best to measure the bed yourself. As a quick reference, though, you can use these sizes:

Crib mattress, 28 x 52in (71 x 132cm); quilt size: 50 x 53in (127 x 134.5cm)

Single-bed mattress, 39 x 75in (99 x 190.5cm); quilt size: 65 x 88in (165 x 223.5cm)

Double-bed mattress, 54 x 75in (137 x 190.5cm); quilt size: 80 x 88in (203 x 223.5cm)

Queen-size mattress, 60 x 80in (152.5 x 203cm); quilt size: 86 x 93in (218.5 x 236cm)

King-size mattress, 76 x 80in (193 x 203cm); quilt size: 104 x 93in (264 x 236cm)

Cuddle-quilt size: 36 x 48in (91.5 x 122cm)

Lap-quilt size: 66 x 76in (167.5 x 193cm)

Even a small quilt will fit a bed. It will sit neatly on top, either square or on point, and is termed a 'topper'. An advantage of this is that it frees you up to stop a quilt when you are ready, or when you run out of fabric! Of course, quilts can also be used as chair throws, picnic rugs and table covers, for which size is less important.

The quickest and easiest way to increase the size of a quilt is to add borders. These do not have to be the same width all the way around. If the quilt design is square, then you can have wider borders on opposite sides in order to make the quilt longer and therefore rectangular in shape. You can have one border in one fabric, or multiple borders in different fabrics and different widths. If you look at 'Ripples' on page 70, you will see that it consists simply of a number of borders around the central square block.

THE PROJECTS

Over the following pages are nine different quilts and matching gifts, all using pre-cut fabric strips in the form of Jelly Rolls™. All the projects can be made in any fabric design you choose, and all make the most of the fact that nearly all the cutting has already been done for you, leaving you to concentrate on the sewing. There are clear, step-by-step instructions and a complete list of the materials and equipment you need for each project. Templates (reproduced actual size) are provided at the back of the book, and there are diagrams to help you with the piecing. So even if you are an absolute beginner, you will be able to tackle all the projects with confidence and make a beautiful quilt of your own.

Ripples 70

Sewing Spools 80

Ohio Star 88

THE GIFTS ...

Humbug Doorstop 48

Spring Door Wreath 56

Book Bag 64

Beach Hut Key Fobs 74

Lavender Stack 84

Woven Dreams 44

Flower Garden 52

Sunny Days 60

Tea Time Treat 98

Autumn Floor 106

Sweet Sixteen 114

Japanese Bag 92

Coffee & Tea Coasters 102

Autumn Cushion 110

Nine-patch Biscornu 118

WOVEN DREAMS

A striking quilt to lay over a single bed or the back of a chair, ready for when the chilly evenings draw in. The red fabric looks like the weft of a fabric being woven on a loom, hence the name of the quilt.

Measurements

Quilt size: 54 x 69in (137 x 175.5cm)
Block size: 8 x 6in (20.5 x 15cm) finished

Fabric requirements

One Jelly Roll™

Fabric for 'wefts': 39½in (1m) Using the same print for these pieces helps give the quilt a coordinated look. Cut six strips 6½in (16.5cm) wide from the width of the fabric. Sub-cut these into rectangles measuring 2½ x 6½in (6.5 x 16.5cm). You will need 81 rectangles altogether.

Backing fabric: 11.5ft (3.5m) Cut into two equal lengths, remove the selvedge and join. Press the seam open.

Wadding: 64 x 79in (162 x 201cm)

Binding: 19¾in (50cm)

Using the same print for the binding and for the 'wefts' helps give the quilt a coordinated look. Cut seven strips 2½in (6.5cm) wide.

METHOD

1 To make the block, simply take two strips of Jelly Roll™ fabric and cut them in half. Use two strips of the same fabric to sandwich a strip of a second fabric. Set the other half of this fabric aside to be sandwiched between another fabric.

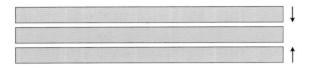

2 Sew the strips together. Press the seams towards the centre strip.

3 Trim off the selvedges and cut three 6½in (16.5cm) squares from the sewn strips.

4 Continue to work your way through the Jelly Roll™ in this way. Using the leftover centre strip from one block as the centre strip in the next one is a good way to work, and avoids odd single strips being left at the end. You need 81 square blocks altogether.

5 Using the 'weft' fabric, stitch a rectangle to one end of each block. Press the seam towards the 'weft' fabric. Repeat this for all the blocks.

6 Lay out the blocks in nine rows, nine blocks in each row. Make sure you have a good mix of colours and patterns over the quilt top. When you are happy with the layout, sew the blocks in each row together. Press all the seams towards the 'weft' fabric.

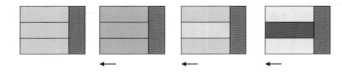

7 When all the rows are sewn, trim 4in (10cm) off the top of four rows and 4in (10cm) off the bottom of five rows, i.e. alternating rows. This will result in a staggered design when you sew the rows together.

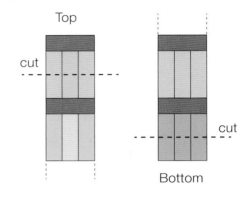

8 Sew the rows together, alternating those that have been trimmed at the top with those that have been trimmed at the bottom. Press all the seams in the same direction.

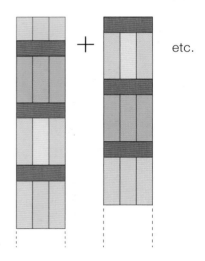

9 Layer the patchwork top with the wadding and backing fabric. Baste together ready for quilting.

10 Quilt the layers. This quilt was machine quilted in a vermicelli design, but see page 34 for other ideas.

11 When the quilt is quilted, bind and label it.

HUMBUG DOORSTOP

This versatile humbug doorstop will prop open doors, keep papers from flying off desks or support books on shelves. The handy handle means you can always get a grip, and take it to where it's needed!

Measurements

6 x 8in (15 x 20.5cm), plus loop

Requirements

For blocks:
Six strips of fabric 2½ x 6½in (6.5 x 16.5cm)
Two strips of fabric 2½ x 6½in (6.5 x 16.5cm) for top
One strip of fabric 2½ x 9in (6.5 x 23cm) for loop handle

Lining:
Calico (muslin), two rectangles 6½ x 8½in (16.5 x 21.5cm)

Filling:
Dried rice, lentils or beans, or birdcage grit, about 17¾oz (500g)

1 Sew two blocks as for the quilt top using the strips of fabric (see page 46).

2 Layer the blocks with the lining fabric, placing them right sides together with the top strip at the top and with the two pieces of calico on the outside.

3 Starting at the top with some securing stitches, sew down the side, across the bottom and up the other side, leaving the top open.

4 Trim the corners and turn the now lined blocks right side out. Push out the corners. Put red thread on the machine, ready for topstitching the handle.

5 To make the handle, fold the strip of fabric in half lengthways, wrong sides together, and press. Now fold and press the raw edges in to meet at the pressed fold.

6 Sew along each long edge of the handle, ⅛in (0.25cm) from the edge.

7 Fill the bag with your chosen filling, to about three-quarters full.

8 Fold the raw edges at the top of the filled doorstop over by ¼in (0.5cm) and pin the handle in place, either side of the side seams. Match the side seams together to pin the opening closed so as to make the characteristic humbug shape.

9 Machine stitch the opening closed, sewing ⅛in (0.25cm) away from the folded edge.

The completed doorstop.

FLOWER GARDEN

I have used a number of different prints for the backgrounds to the blocks, adding to the floweriness of the quilt! Some of the prints are floral while others have a dotty design that reminds me of seeds in the wind. Choose the same fabric for the backgrounds for a more coordinated look.

Measurements

Quilt size: 72 x 72in (183 x 183cm)

Block size: 18½ x 18½in (47 x 47cm)

Fabric requirements

Flowers: One Jelly Roll™

Flower centres: 11¾in (30cm)

Backgrounds for the blocks: 13ft (4m) or 16 fat quarters Cut sixteen squares measuring 16½ x 16½in (42 x 42cm).

Frames: 4½ft (1.4m) Cut one piece 16½in (42cm) wide. Sub-cut this into 3in (7.5cm) strips. This will yield fourteen strips. Cut two pieces 18½in (47cm) wide. Layer on top of each other and sub-cut into a total of sixteen 3in (7.5cm) strips. Using the remaining fabric, trim to 16½in (42cm) and sub-cut into 3in (7.5cm) strips. You need two to complete the total of sixteen 16½in (42cm) wide strips needed for the quilt blocks.

Backing fabric: 14ft (4.3m) Cut into two equal lengths, remove selvedges and join together lengthways. Press the seam open.

Wadding: 82 x 82in (208.5cm)

Binding: 21½in (55cm) Cut eight strips 2½in (6.5cm) wide.

Tools: Creative Grids® 18° circle segment ruler or templates for flower centre and petals (see page 126)

Freezer paper for appliqué

METHOD

1 To make the flowers, trim off the selvedge and cut the Jelly Roll™ strips into 5in (13cm) segments. You will get eight from each strip, 320 in total. Using the circle segment ruler or the petal template (page 126), trim the segments to the required shape.

2 Fold each segment in half lengthways with right sides facing. Stitch across the top taking a ¼in (0.5cm) seam allowance. If you are using a sewing machine, use the chain-piecing method (page 19).

3 Snip ⅛in (0.25cm) off the seam allowance at the fold to reduce bulk, and turn the tip of the petal right side out. Press flat.

4 Arrange the petals in groups of twenty per flower to create sixteen flowers.

5 Stitch the petals together, starting at the folded edge to ensure accuracy. If the petals are not aligned properly in the middle, it will not matter too much as this will be covered with the appliqué centre. Press all the seams in one direction.

6 To prepare a background square for the flower to be sewn on to, fold it into quarters and finger press.

7 Lay the flower face up on the front of the square, lining up the quarter marks with the petals. At every five petals there will be a quarter mark on the background fabric.

8 Pin the flower in place at the circumference and attach it using appliqué stitch (see page 22).

9 Prepare sixteen circles for the flower centres following the instructions on page 22. Use the template on page 126.

10 Fold each circle into quarters and crease at the circumference.

11 Place a circle in the centre of a flower by lining up the creases with the quarter seams of the flower (every five petals). Pin the circle in place and appliqué down (see pages 22–23). Make sixteen flower blocks altogether.

The back of a flower, showing all the petals stitched together and the seams pressed.

12 Sew a short – 16½in (42cm) – framing strip to one side of each of the blocks. Press the seam towards the framing strip.

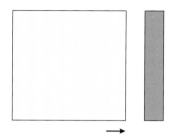

13 Sew a long – 18½in (47cm) – framing strip to an adjacent side on each block. Press the seam towards the strip.

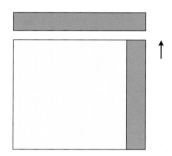

14 Lay out the blocks in four rows, four blocks in each row, turning the blocks as shown in the diagram.

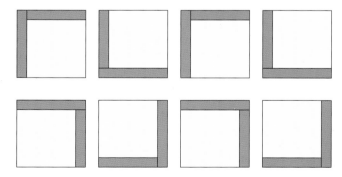

15 Sew the blocks together to make rows, retaining the arrangement shown in the diagram above. Press the seams in alternating directions on each row.

16 Sew the rows together. Press the seams in one direction.

17 Layer the quilt with wadding and backing fabric. Baste together ready for quilting. I used a cross-hatch quilting design, but any quilting method can be used (see pages 34–35).

18 Complete the quilt by binding and labelling.

SPRING DOOR WREATH

Look forward to the coming of spring with this colourful door wreath, although it would make a welcoming addition to your home at any time of the year. Choose different fabrics to reflect the different seasons – oranges, reds and browns for an autumnal feel and perhaps white, cream and silver for Christmas.

Measurements

10in (25.5cm) across

Requirements

One polystyrene ring, 9¾in (25cm) diameter

Fabric glue

To wrap the wreath:
Oddments of Jelly Rolls™ approximately 2½ x 6in (6.5 x 15cm)
Join 31 together to form a continuous length of 15½ft (4.75m). Use a smaller-than-usual sewing machine stitch to prevent the seams unravelling. Wind into a loose bundle to make it easier to work with.

Flowers:
Oddments of Jelly Rolls™
For outer petals: 2½ x 9in (6.5 x 23cm)
For inner petals: 2½ x 7in (6.5 x 18cm)

Buttons: ½–¾in (1.5–2cm) diameter, one for each flower

2in (5cm) felt squares

Loop for hanging:
One Jelly Roll™ strip

1 Glue the wrong side of the end of the long piece of fabric to the wreath and temporarily secure it with a pin. Wind the fabric around the wreath, overlapping the edges to cover the wreath. When you reach the start, trim and glue the end, using the pin to secure it. Remove the pin when the glue is completely dry.

2 To make the loop, trim the selvedge from the Jelly Roll™ strip with pinking shears for a decorative effect. Tie these ends into a knot. Loop through the wreath and then through the loop itself and pull tight. Position the loop over the fabric join on the wreath.

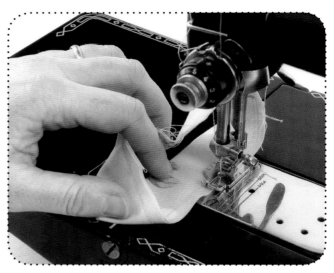

3 The inner and outer flower petals are made in the same way and layered one on top of the other. Take a strip of fabric, fold it in half lengthways and press. Unfold the fabric and then sew the two ends together to form a continuous loop. Press the seam open.

4 Fold the loop with wrong sides facing and press. With the machine on its longest stitch setting, sew around the loop ⅛in (0.25cm) from the raw edge. Do this without securing the stitches at the end of the row, and without overlapping the start of the row. Cut off the threads, leaving a long tail thread. Sew another row of long stitches between the first row and the raw edge. Finish in the same way.

5 At one end of the two rows of stitching, tie the threads together to secure. At the other end, use the two top threads only to carefully gather up the loop to create the flower petals. Tie off the threads with a secure knot and trim.

6 Lay the inner petals upside down and place the outer petals upside down on top, then lay a felt square on top of that.

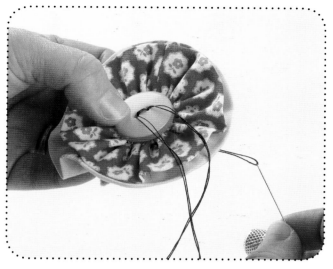

7 Turn the layered flower over and place a button in the centre. Stitch the button in place using a doubled thread in a contrasting colour, and taking the thread through all the layers of the flower to secure them.

The completed flower.

8 Glue the felt backing to the wreath wherever you think the flower looks good.

9 Add as many flower, in various colour combinations, as you like.

SUNNY DAYS

Not all quilts are destined for the lounge or the bedroom. This one has a bright and happy feel that makes me want to bundle it into a bicycle basket on a warm, sunny day, sling the book bag over my shoulder and cycle off to the beach to have a good read with a comfy quilt to lay on.

Measurements

Quilt size: 65 x 78in (165 x 198cm)
Block size: 13 x 13in (33 x 33cm) finished

Fabric requirements

Frames: One Jelly Roll™

Centre squares: 9½ft (2.9m), in total, of assorted pale fabrics Cut 120 squares measuring 5 x 5in (13 x 13cm), or use ready-cut charm squares.

Backing fabric: 12¾ft (3.9m) Cut into two equal lengths, remove selvedges and join together lengthwise. Press the seam open.

Wadding: 75 x 88in (190.5 x 223.5cm)

Binding: 21½in (55cm) Cut eight strips 2½in (6.5cm) wide.

METHOD

Make 120 blocks in total, using either method 1 or method 2 below.

Method 1

1 Attach the fabric squares to the Jelly Roll™ strips using a variation of the sew-and-cut technique (see page 20). Take a Jelly Roll™ strip, trim off the selvedge and place the trimmed edge under the machine, right side up, ready to stitch. Now place a 5in (13cm) square on top, right sides facing, align the raw edges of the seam and sew to the end of the square. Leave ¼in (0.5cm) of strip and then add another square and sew in the same way.

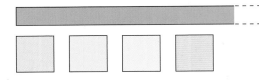

2 Continue adding squares until the strip is full. You should fit about eight squares on to a Jelly Roll™ strip. Remove the fabric from the machine and cut through the strip between the squares. Press the seams towards the Jelly Roll™ strip.

> ### Note
> For more variation in fabric combinations, cut the strips in half first.

3 Take another Jelly Roll™ strip, cut off the selvedge and place it under the machine ready to sew, right side up, as before. On top of the strip, place one of the rectangles you have just stitched, right sides facing, with the cut edge of the strip aligned with the raw edge of the Jelly Roll™ strip. Stitch as before. You will fit about six of these on to the strip. Cut off each of the newly stitched squares as you did before. Press the seams to the square.

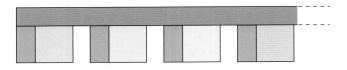

Method 2

1 If you prefer to cut the Jelly Roll™ strips first, then cut 120 pieces measuring 2½ x 5in (6.5 x 13cm) and 120 pieces measuring 2½ x 7in (6.5 x 18cm). Stitch a 5in (13cm) rectangle to a square. Press the seams towards the strip.

2 Sew a 7in (18cm) strip to the side of the rectangle. Press the seams towards the square.

Assembling the patchwork

1 Lay out the blocks in groups of four, as in the diagram below.

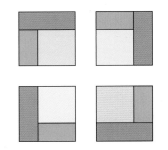

> ### Note
> Remember to use different combinations of fabrics and colours to achieve a good mix in your finished design.

2 Sew the blocks together in pairs, as shown in the diagram, and press the seams of each pair in opposite directions.

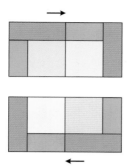

3 Sew the two pairs together and press the seams open. Make 30 of these larger blocks altogether.

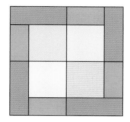

4 Lay out the blocks for the quilt, five blocks across and six down.

5 Sew the blocks together in each row, pressing the seams in alternating directions on each row.

6 Sew the rows together, pressing all the seams in the same direction.

7 Lay the patchwork out and baste it together with the backing and wadding.

8 I have used the Amish wave design for the quilting (see page 35) but any quilting design can be used instead. Big-stitch quilting works very well, and I have used this on the book bag on pages 64–65.

9 Bind and label the quilt to finish (see pages 36–40).

BOOK BAG

Use two of the blocks from the quilt to stitch this easy-to-make bag to hold your books and magazines when you're out and about.

Measurements

Bag: 13in (33cm) square
Straps: 21in (53.5cm) long

Requirements

Two patchwork blocks from the Sunny Days quilt

Wadding:
15 x 30in (38 x 76cm)

Calico (muslin):
15 x 30in (38 x 76cm)

Quilting thread:
Valdani pearl cotton no. 8

Lining fabric:
13½ x 26½in (34 x 67cm)

Handles:
Two strips of lining fabric, 2½ x 42in (6.5 x 106.5cm)
Two Jelly Roll™ strips

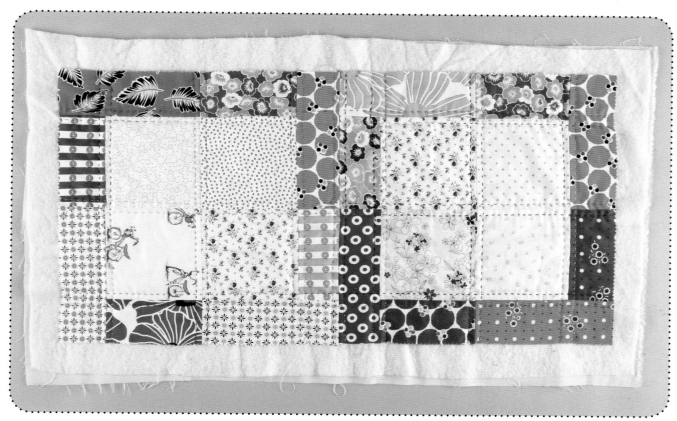

1 Stitch two blocks as for the quilt (see pages 62–63). Sew them together to form a rectangle. Layer and baste them together with the calico (muslin) and wadding. Outline the shapes using big-stitch quilting for a fun, bold effect (see page 32). Trim the surplus wadding and calico from around the edges.

2 Fold the bag in half, right sides together, align the sides and pin them in place. Stitch along the seams.

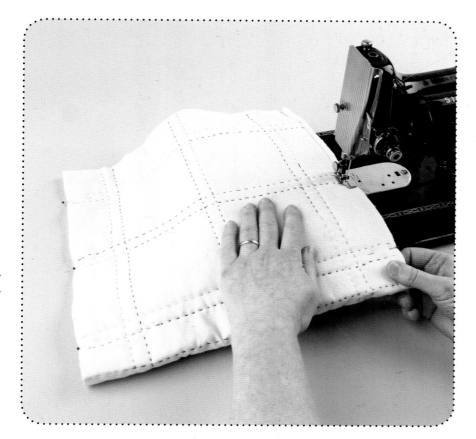

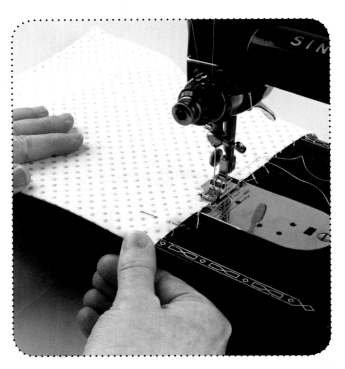

3 Fold the lining fabric in half in the same way, wrong sides facing, pin and stitch the side seams. Leave a 4in (10cm) gap in the middle of one of the seams.

4 For each strap, lay a Jelly Roll™ strip on top of a strip of lining fabric, right sides facing, and align the edges. Stitch down one side.

5 Press the raw edges in to meet at the seam along the entire length, wrong sides together.

6 Change to a contrasting thread, fold the strap in half along the seam, and stitch down both sides ⅛in (0.25cm) from the edge. Make two straps and trim them both to the same length.

7 Pin a straps to each side of the bag, as shown in the photograph, using the patches to position them accurately. Align the top and bottom edge of each strap with the top of the bag, and lay them with the lining fabric uppermost. Stay stitch the straps in place.

The straps are attached to the bag so that the Jelly Roll™ fabric is on the outside.

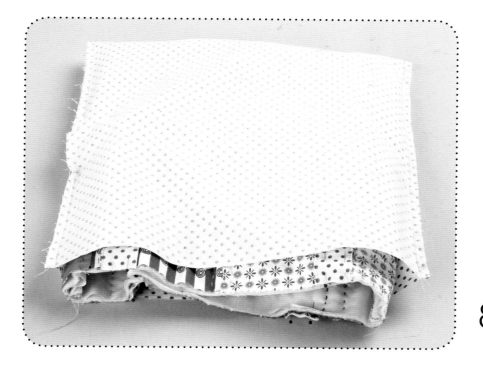

8 With the lining still inside out, place the bag in the lining.

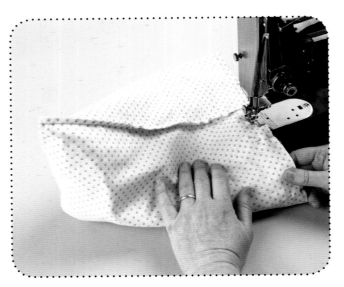

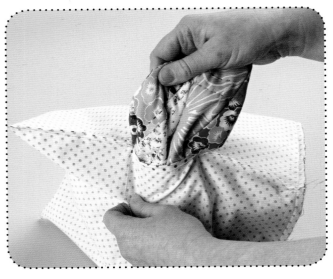

9 Sew around the top edge of the bag, securing the lining and the straps. Remove the pins as you go. Overlap the start of the stitch line when you reach the end to secure the stitching.

10 Turn the bag right side out through the hole left in the lining seam. Slipstitch the hole in the lining closed.

11 Push the lining inside the bag and roll the top of the lining so that approximately ½in (1cm) is visible at the top of the bag. Pin the lining in place and stitch 'in the ditch' from the front of the bag to secure the lining and trim the top of the bag.

The finished bag.

RIPPLES

The design of this quilt spreads from the centre outwards, hence the name 'ripples'. The blues and greens that dominate the colour selection add to the watery theme, creating a quilt that is reminiscent of a tropical sea – perfect for taking to the beach on a hot summer's day!

Measurements

Quilt size: 68 x 68in (172.5 x 172.5cm) with borders; 54 x 54in (137 x 137cm) without borders

Fabric requirements

One Jelly Roll™

Centre square: One fat quarter

Borders: 15¾in (40cm) of each of four different fabrics
From each fabric cut two 7in (18cm) wide strips, trim the selvedges and join. Press the seams open.

Backing fabric: 13ft (4m)
Cut into two equal lengths, remove selvedges and join. Press the seam open.

Wadding: 78 x 78in (198 x 198cm)

Binding: 19.5in (50cm)
Cut seven strips 2½in (6.5cm) wide

Tools: Creative Grids® quarter-square triangle ruler or similar, or the template on page 124

METHOD

1 Cut one 8½in (21.5cm) square from the fat quarter to use as the centre of the quilt.

2 From the Jelly Roll™, cut thirty of the strips in half so they are each about 20in (51cm) long.

3 Select eight of the short strips and, using the template on page 124 or the specialist ruler, cut 56 quarter-square triangles. Each 20in (51cm) strip will yield seven triangles.

4 Sew three triangles together, as in the diagram below, and press all the seams in the same direction. Offset the triangles slightly to create a seam allowance for when the rows of triangles are sewn to the centre square. Make four of these.

5 Sew two triangles together, as in the diagram below, and press the seam open. Make four of these.

6 Lay out the triangles to surround the centre square.

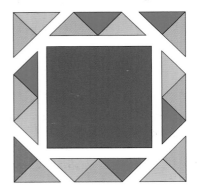

7 Mark the centre of one side of the square by finger pressing and match this to the centre of one row of triangles. Attach the row of triangles to the square. Press the seams towards the square.

8 Sew on the row of triangles on the opposite side of the square and press the seam towards the centre. Sew on the remaining two rows and, again, press the seams towards the centre.

9 Sew the four corners to the block, matching the seams to the corners. Press the seams open.

10 Take the remaining Jelly Roll™ strips and trim off the selvedge ends. Join the strips to form one continuous strip, mixing up the patterns and fabric lengths. Press the seams open.

11 Join the remaining triangles together to make six rows of five or seven triangles, as in step 4. Press all the seams in one direction.

12 Take the long strip of fabric you made in step 10, align the end with one edge of the block and sew it along one side of the block. Trim it off when you reach the end. Do the same on the opposite side of the block. Press the seams away from the centre.

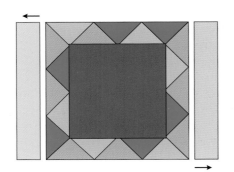

13 Repeat on the remaining opposite sides of the block. Press the seams away from the centre.

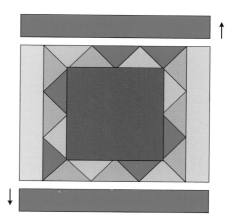

14 Continue to build up the quilt in this way, adding strips to opposite sides of the centre block.

15 At various points, six in total, insert a row of triangles into the quilt. To join the triangles to the fabric strip, trim the end of the fabric strip using the template or the specialist cutting ruler, then stitch the triangle row to the strip of fabric as shown in the diagram. Remember to offset the strip as you did in step 4. Press the seam towards the strip.

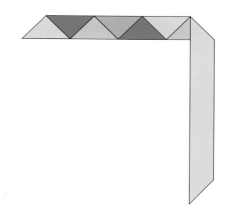

16 When you have completed the patchwork it should measure approximately 54in (137in) square. You can now add a border.

17 Stitch strips of border fabric to opposite sides of the patchwork, trimming off the excess at the edges. Press the seams towards the border. Repeat on the remaining two sides.

18 Layer and baste the quilt together ready for quilting.

19 I have used vermicelli quilting. See pages 34–35 for some other ideas.

20 Bind and label your quilt (see pages 36–40).

BEACH HUT KEY FOBS

You'll never lose your keys again with these pretty key fobs
– and they look gorgeous too. Try using colours or fabrics to
match the doors they open, or suit the owner of the key.

Measurements

4 x 4in (10 x 10cm) plus loop

Requirements

Fabric for house:
One square 2½ x 2½in
(6.5 x 6.5cm)
One rectangle 2½ x 4½in
(6.5 x 11.5cm)

Fabric for background:
Two squares 2½in (6.5cm)
Two rectangles 2½ x 1½in
(6.5 x 4cm)

Backing and loop:
One square 5 x 5in (13 x 13cm)
One strip 1¼ x 2½in
(3 x 6.5cm)

Wadding:
One square 5 x 5in (13 x 13cm)

Quilting thread:
Valdani pearl cotton no. 8

Metal key ring

1 To make the house, stitch a rectangle of the background fabric to each side of the square of house fabric, right sides facing. Press the seams towards the square.

2 For the roof, take a square of background fabric and draw a diagonal line on the back. Lay it at one end of the house-fabric rectangle, right sides facing, as shown above. Stitch along the diagonal line.

3 Trim off the triangle, leaving a ¼in (0.5cm) seam allowance. Press, with the seam towards the house fabric.

4 Repeat on the other side of the rectangle.

5 Lay the roof on top of the house, right sides facing, and stitch them together. Press the seam towards the house.

6 Lay the house on top of the square of backing fabric, right sides together, and place them on the wadding.

7 Make the loop from the fabric strip. Fold it in half lengthways, wrong sides together, and press. Unfold, then fold the raw edges in towards the fold line. Fold in half and press again.

8 Stitch down the open side to secure, about ⅛in (0.25cm) from the edge.

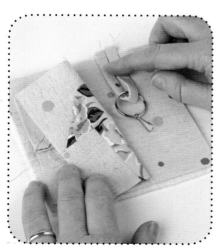

9 Thread the loop through the key ring and position it between the two layers of fabric, as shown above. Make sure it lies to one side of the roof.

10 Pin the layers in place and stitch around the house block, stitching diagonally across the corners, as shown. Leave a 1½in (4cm) gap in the stitching on one side for turning through.

11 Trim off the corners and the excess backing fabric and wadding.

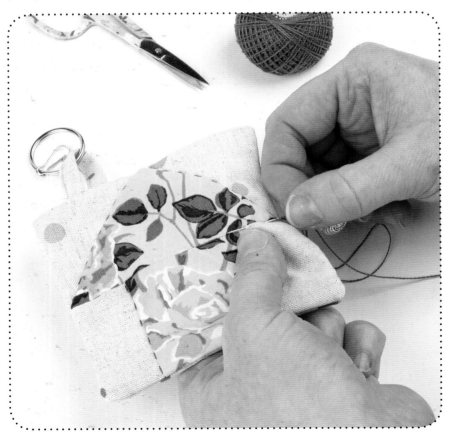

12 Turn right side out and slipstitch the opening closed. Use big-stitch quilting to quilt the layers together, stitching around the outline of the house. You can also embroider on a door and windows using backstitch, stitching through all the layers.

SEWING SPOOLS

These simple repeat blocks remind me of old-fashioned sewing-thread spools. I tried to use a dark fabric for the centre of each spool, and worked the tops and bottoms in the same fabric. Play around with your strips and see what combinations work for you. The lighter background fabric could all be in one design, but for a less formal look choose similar fabrics but with different patterns.

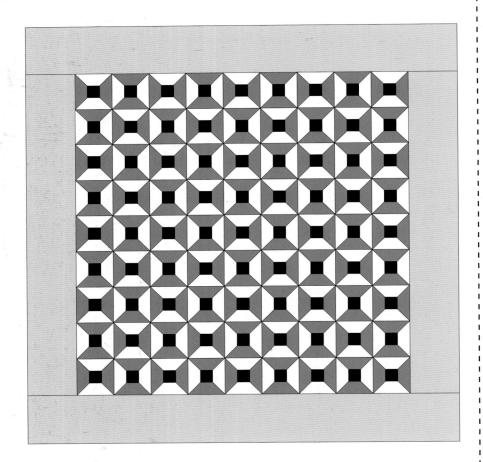

Measurements

Quilt size: 70 x 70in (178 x 178cm)
Block size: 6 x 6in (15 x 15cm) finished

Fabric requirements

Fabric for 'spools':
One Jelly Roll™.
Cut 162 rectangles measuring 2½ x 7¼in (6.5 x 18.5cm). Alternatively, use the template on page 124 and do not pre-cut into rectangles. For the centres, cut 81 squares each 2½ x 2½in (6.5 x 6.5cm). Each strip should yield either 5 rectangles and 1 square or 4 rectangles and 4 squares. You may want to select certain fabrics for the spool centres and keep the rest for the tops and bottoms.

Background fabric: 7½ft (2.25m)
Cut into 162 rectangles measuring 2½ x 7¼in (6.5 x 18.5cm). Alternatively, use the template on page 124 and do not pre-cut into rectangles; cut into 17 strips 2½in (6.5cm) wide instead.

Border: 4½ft (1.4m)
Cut six strips 8½in (21.5cm) wide. Remove selvedge, join to make a continuous length and press the seams open.

Backing fabric: 14ft (4.2m)
Cut into two equal lengths, remove selvedges and join. Press the seams open.

Wadding: 80 x 80in (203 x 203cm)

Binding: 21¾in (55cm)
Cut into eight strips 2½in (6.5cm) wide.

Tools: half-square triangle ruler or similar, or use the 45° line on your cutting mat.

METHOD

1 Use the template on page 124 or the 45° angle on a specialist ruler to trim the corners from all the rectangles.

Alternatively, to avoid wastage, use the template to cut the shapes from a continuous strip of fabric.

2 Sew the top and bottom of each spool to the centre square, starting and stopping ¼in (0.5cm) away from the edge. Press the seams open. This will help you set the design in the background fabric.

3 Place one of the background shapes on top of one end of the spool, lining them up exactly, right sides together. Sew, with the background fabric flat on the bed of the sewing machine, up towards the centre of the block.

4 When you reach the open seam, stop with the needle in the work, lift the foot and pivot the centre of the spool block through 90° so that the edge lines up with the corresponding edge of the background shape. Replace the presser foot and stitch to the next open seam.

5 Repeat step 4, stitching down the side of the spool.

6 Repeat steps 3 to 5 on the other side of the spool. Press the seams towards the spool.

7 Stitch 81 blocks in total.

8 Lay the blocks out in nine rows of nine blocks. Alternate the direction of the spools, as shown in the diagram below.

9 Sew the blocks together in rows, pressing the seams towards the spool fabric.

10 Sew the rows together and press the seams open.

11 Cut two strips from the border fabric, each 54½in (138.5cm) long and sew them to opposite sides of the quilt. Press the seams towards the border.

12 Cut two strips of border fabric each 70½in (179cm) long and sew them to the remaining two sides, again pressing the seams towards the border.

13 Layer the quilt top with the backing and wadding, and baste them together ready to quilt.

14 The quilting design I used was vermicelli, but any of the designs shown on pages 34–35 are suitable.

15 After quilting, remove the basting and bind and label the quilt (see pages 36–40).

LAVENDER STACK

I love to place these in drawers and linen cupboards to freshen everything with the scent of lavender. A stack of two or three pillows tied together makes a lovely gift. To make them into pincushions, omit the lavender bags and fill with bran or birdcage grit, as this will help sharpen your pins when they are pushed and pulled through the cushion.

Measurements

Each cushion is 6in (15cm) square

Requirements

One 'spools' block per cushion from the Sewing Spools quilt

Wadding:
One 8in (20.5cm) square

Lining:
One 8in (20.5cm) square

Backing:
6½in (16.5cm) square

Lavender pouches:
One 6 x 3in (15 x 7.5cm) rectangle of calico (muslin)
Dried lavender

Polyester filling

Ribbon or tape (optional)

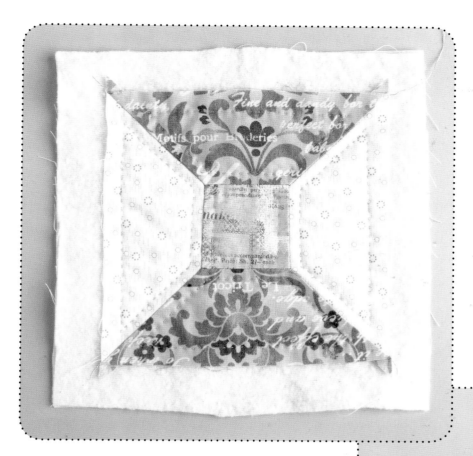

1 Sew the spools block. Layer it with a square of wadding and lining and baste the layers together. Outline quilt around the shapes, ¼in (0.5cm) from the seams and ½in (1cm) from the raw edges, using little-stitch quilting (see page 32). Trim the wadding and lining fabric to the block size.

2 Lay the quilted block in the middle of the backing fabric, right sides together. Pin them together. Starting in the middle of one side, sew a ¼in (0.5cm) seam allowance all around the edge of the block, leaving a 1½in (4cm) gap to turn through. Sew diagonally across the corners to get a better finish.

The quilted block attached to the backing fabric, before being turned out.

3 Trim off the seam allowances at the corners to reduce bulk.

4 Turn the cushion right side out through the gap and stuff with polyester filling.

5 Fold the rectangle of calico (muslin) in half and stitch along two sides to form a square pouch.

6 Fill the pouch with dried lavender.

7 Stitch across the top of the pouch, either by machine or by hand, insert it in the cushion and sew up the gap.

Make two or three cushions and tie them together with tape or, for a more feminine feel, silk ribbon.

OHIO STAR

This dramatic quilt is quick to stitch, and makes the most of your favourite fabrics. To show off the star to its best advantage, surround it with a plain or pale fabric. The diagonal corners are a striking feature of this quilt, but if you would rather have a 'square' quilt, cut four 6½in (16.5cm) squares and follow the method for the border of the Autumn Floor quilt on page 106.

Measurements

Quilt size: 70 x 70in (178 x 178cm)

Fabric requirements

Star and border: One Jelly Roll™

Background: 4ft (1.2m) Cut four squares measuring 20½ x 20½in (52 x 52cm) for the corners. Cut one square measuring 21¾ x 21¾in (55 x 55cm). Cut this square into four quarter-square triangles.

Backing fabric: 13¾ft (4.2m) Cut into two equal lengths, remove selvedges and join. Press the seams open.

Wadding: 80 x 80in (203 x 203cm)

Binding: 21½in (55cm). Cut eight strips 2½in (6.5cm) wide

METHOD

1 Select 20 Jelly Roll™ strips for the star. Sort them into two groups of ten fabrics.

2 Sew the fabric strips in one group together to form one piece. Remember to sew from opposite ends of the strips on each row to avoid distortion. Press the seams in one direction. Repeat for the second set of strips.

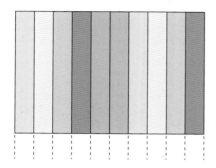

3 Trim off the selvedges and cut two 20½in (52cm) squares from each piece. This will give you four squares in total.

4 Cut each square diagonally into four triangles.

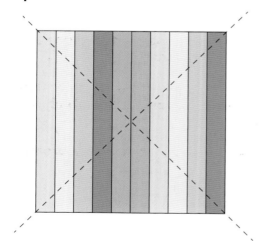

5 Lay out the triangles as shown in the diagram below. Note the direction of the strips. You will see the star starting to take shape.

6 Sew the triangles that form the four centre squares together first. Press the seams open. Handle the fabric carefully as all of the outside edges of the squares are on the bias and will stretch easily.

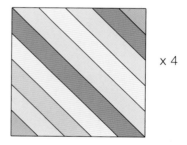

x 4

7 Stitch each of the four background triangles to a star point as shown below. Press the seams towards the background fabric.

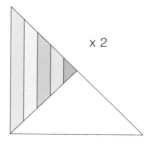

x 2

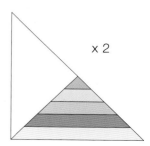

x 2

8 Take two background squares and sew two of these sections to each one as shown below. Press the seams to the background fabric.

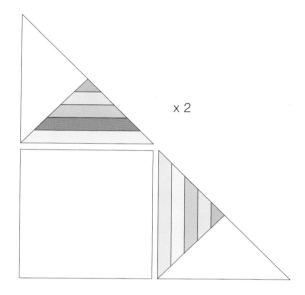

x 2

9 Sew the remaining star points to the other two background squares, as shown below. Press the seams to the background fabric.

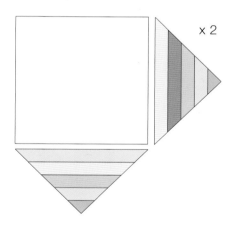

x 2

10 Stitch these two smaller units to the central square, on opposite sides, following the diagram on page 88 for guidance. Press the seams to the centre square.

11 Now attach the remaining larger units that you made in step 8 to complete the star. Press the seams away from the centre.

12 Sew the remaining 20 Jelly Roll™ strips together along their lengths, as you did in step 2. Press the seams in one direction.

13 Trim off the selvedge. Cut the fabric into six 6½in (16.5cm) sections.

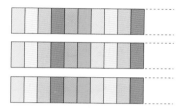

14 Join the sections to form one long continuous length for the border.

15 You will need a border of 30 strips for each side of the quilt. Count along 30 strips from the end and separate the sections at this point by unpicking the seam. Continue along in this way to make four borders, each consisting of 30 strips.

16 Sew the border to each side of the quilt. Press the seams towards the quilt centre. At the corners, use the 45° angle on your cutting mat to trim off the excess.

17 Layer and baste the top with the wadding and backing fabric ready to quilt.

18 Quilt using either the vermicelli design, as I have, or any of the other quilting designs shown on pages 34–35.

19 Bind and label the quilt to complete (see pages 36–40).

JAPANESE BAG

This simple bag folds up easily to store away in a pocket, handbag or purse. Just unfold it, knot the handles together and your bag is ready to go. This is based on a typical Japanese design, with a tweak or two to help you sew it quickly.

Measurements

28 x 28in (71 x 71cm)

Requirements

Ten Jelly Roll™ strips, 2½in (6.5cm) wide

One square of coordinating fabric, 20½ x 20½in (52 x 52cm)

Lining: 20½ x 60½in (52 x 153.5cm)

Quilting thread: Valdani pearl cotton no. 12, for topstitching the edge

1 Sew all the strips together along their length. Press the seams in one direction and trim off the selvedge. Cut two squares 20½ x 20½in (52 x 52cm).

2 Stitch a square to either side of the square of coordinating fabric. Press the seams towards the solid fabric square.

The two squares cut from the stitched Jelly Roll™ strips, attached to the square of coordinating fabric.

3 Place the fabric right side up on a flat surface. Fold the left-hand panel over on to the centre panel and pin the top edges together.

4 Stitch along the top edge: secure with two or three backstitches at the fold and stitch towards the free edge, stopping ¼in (0.5cm) before the edge; secure with backstitches. Lay the fabric out again and fold the top layer away from the bottom edge.

5 Fold the righ-hand panel over on to the left-hand panel and pin it in place along the bottom edge. Stitch the bottom seam, as you did the top seam.

Note

Make sure you stitch through two layers only – the right-hand panel and the centre panel – the left-hand panel should be lifted away.

6 Pull up the two free corners to make the bag shape.

7 Lay out the lining fabric, and fold and stitch it in the same way to create a second bag. Leave a 4in (10cm) gap in one of the seams for turning through. Press the seams away from the centre panel.

8 Turn the lining the right way out and place it in the bag, right sides together. Match the seams and align the raw edges. Pin them in place.

9 Sew around all the raw edges, starting on the long edge of a strip. Take two or three stitches diagonally across the corners and across the bottom of the 'V'. When you have finished stitching, clip the corners to achieve a neater finish when you turn the bag out.

10 Turn the bag right side out through the gap in the lining and slipstitch the gap closed. Roll the edge of the bag between your fingers before pressing the seam to ensure that the lining is not exposed on the front of the bag.

11 Use big-stitch quilting and the pearl cotton to secure the edge ¼in (0.5cm) from the seam (see page 32).

To use the bag, tie the two end in a square knot to create the handle. When the bag is not in use, untie the knot and fold the bag down into a flat square for easy storage.

TEA TIME TREAT

This quilt would look great for a sunny summer picnic, or draped over a table for alfresco dining. Use up leftover triangles for the coasters (see page 102) to stand your tea or coffee pot on.

Measurements

Quilt size: 65 x 65in (165 x 165cm)
Block size: 8in (20.5cm) finished size

Fabric requirements

One Jelly Roll™

Sashing and block centres: Calico (muslin), 6ft (1.8m) For the block centres, cut four strips 4½in (11.5cm) wide. Sub-cut these into 4½in (11.5cm) squares. You will need 36 squares altogether. For the sashing, cut three strips 16½in (42cm) wide. Sub-cut these into rectangles measuring 4½ x 16½in (11.5 x 42cm). You will need 24 of these.

Backing fabric: 12¾ft (3.9m) Cut into two equal lengths, remove selvedges and join. Press the seams open.

Wadding: 75 x 75in (190.5 x 190.5cm)

Binding: 19½in (50cm) Cut seven strips 2½in (6.5cm) wide.

Tools: quarter-square triangle specialist ruler or template on page 124.

METHOD

1 Using the template (page 124) or the quarter-square triangle ruler, cut the Jelly Roll™ strips into triangles. Each strip should yield about 14 triangles. You will need around 500 for the quilt, but will probably cut around 560 from all of the strips. This will allow you to be selective about which you use, and there will be some extra for the coasters project on page 102.

2 To start sewing the triangles to the centre squares, you will need to find the middle of each side of each square. Simply fold each square into quarters and finger press at the outside edge. Do the same to the long side of each triangle before you sew it to the square, aligning the centre marks before stitching. This will help keep everything centred and the sewing even.

3 Using these centre marks, sew a triangle to opposite sides of the square. Press the seams.

4 Now add a triangle to the two remaining opposite sides of the square. Press the seams. Repeat for all of the squares.

5 To make the corner units sew two triangles together along their short sides. You will need 144 units, so you may want to use chain piecing here (see page 19). Press the seams open.

6 Sew these units to opposite sides of the block. Align the seams with the corners of the centre square. Press.

7 Now add the remaining units to the opposite sides of the block. Press. Repeat for all of the blocks.

8 Lay the blocks out in nine groups of four, as shown.

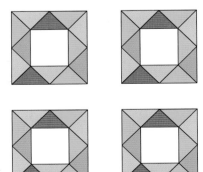

9 Sew the blocks together in pairs, press the seams, then sew the pairs together. Press. Make nine of these four-block units.

10 To make the posts, sew triangles together as for step 5. Make 32 of these units, then sew them together to make squares. Press.

11 Lay out the units in three rows of three. Add a sashing strip between each unit and one at either end, as in the diagram on page 98. Sew these together into rows and press the seams towards the sashing strips.

12 Lay out sashing strips and corner posts between these rows, starting and stopping with a post. Make four of these rows, two to join the three rows of units, and two to go at the top and bottom of the quilt. Press the seams towards the sashing.

13 Sew all the rows of the quilt together. Press the seams towards the sashing.

14 Layer and baste the top with the wadding and backing fabric ready to quilt.

15 Quilt using any of the quilting designs shown on pages 34–35.

16 Bind and label the quilt to complete (see pages 36–40).

COFFEE AND TEA COASTERS

Make these colourful coasters to go with your quilt, or make extra ones and give a set to a friend. The coasters' generous size means there is room for a biscuit too, and no crumbs on the table!

Measurements

Coaster size:
Small: 6in (15cm) square
Large: 8in (20.5cm) square

Requirements

Centres:
One square of calico (muslin), 4½ x 4½in (11.5 x 11.5cm), per coaster

Triangles:
Small coaster: four triangles
Large coaster: twelve triangles Cut triangles using the template (page 124) or a quarter-square triangle specialist ruler.

Valdani pearl cotton no. 8

Wadding:
Use a heat-resistant wadding to protect your surfaces.
Small coaster: 8in (20.5cm) square
Large coaster: 10in (25.5cm) square

Backing fabric:
Small coaster: 8in (20.5cm) square
Large coaster: 10in (25.5cm) square

Binding: Four strips of fabric, each 2½in (6.5cm) wide, or Jelly Roll™ strips, and long enough for each side of the coasters – approximately 10–12in (25.5–30.5cm).

Spray glue (optional)

Note

The instructions on the following pages are for the small coaster. To make the large version, follow the same steps but start with the larger quilt block (i.e. follow the quilt instructions up to step 7).

1 For a small coaster, make a quilt block following the quilt instructions up to step 4. Layer it with an 8in (20.5cm) square of wadding and an 8in (20.5cm) square of backing fabric. Spray glue or tack the layers together, if you wish. Mark on the centre line using an acrylic ruler and a Hera marker.

2 Quilt along the marked line.

3 Continue to quilt in parallel lines across the coaster. Use the width of the presser foot as a guide to space the lines evenly.

4 Fold a 2½in (6.5cm) wide strip of fabric in half lengthways, wrong sides facing, and press. Align the raw edges with one edge of the coaster and stitch it in place. Stitch a strip to the opposite side of the coaster too. (See square-cornered binding, page 39.)

5 Trim the excess wadding and backing fabric from the sides with the binding.

6 Attach binding to the remaining two opposite sides in the same way, overlapping the first binding strips at both ends. Use a contrasting fabric. Again, trim off the excess wadding and backing fabric.

7 Turn the coaster over with the back uppermost and snip off the corners.

8 Fold over the binding to the back of the work and pin then slipstitch it in place.

AUTUMN FLOOR

The colours in this quilt reminded me of a woodland floor in the autumn, carpeted with fallen leaves. Depending on your fabric choice, it could just as easily be a 'spring floor' with mosses and wild flowers. Experiment, and see what your fabric selection conjures up in your imagination.

Measurements

Quilt size: 69 x 69in (175 x 175cm)
Block size: 18in (46cm) finished

Fabric requirements

One Jelly Roll™

Sashing fabric: 27½in (70cm) Use either the same fabric or, for more variety, try combining different fabrics. Cut three strips 8½in (21.5cm) wide. Subcut these into 2½in (6.5cm) wide rectangles. You need 36 rectangles in total.

Posts and border corners: 11¾in (30cm). Cut one strip 2½in (6.5cm) wide and sub-cut this into nine 2½in (6.5cm) squares for the posts. Cut another strip 7½in (19cm) wide and sub-cut this into four 7½in (19cm) squares for the border corners.

Border: 4ft (1.2m) Use either the same fabric as that used for the sashing or, for more variety, a combination of different fabrics. Cut six strips 7½in (19cm) wide. Remove the selvedges and join to make one long, continuous strip. Press the seams open.

Backing fabric: 13ft (4m). Cut into two equal lengths, remove the selvedges and join lengthways. Press the seams open.

Wadding: 79 x 79in (200.5 x 200.5cm)

Binding: 19½in (50cm) Cut seven strips 2½in (6.5cm) wide.

METHOD

1 Divide the Jelly Roll™ strips into ten groups of four. You only need nine of these to make the quilt blocks, so you can use the remaining one for the matching cushion on page 110.

2 Stitch the four strips in each group together. Alternate the ends from which you start to sew to avoid fabric distortion. Press all the seams in one direction.

3 Trim off the selvedge. Cut the fabric into four 8½in (21.5cm) squares.

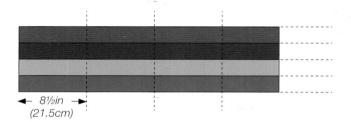

8½in
(21.5cm)

4 Lay out the squares in groups of four with lengths of sashing between them and a post in the middle, as in the diagram below.

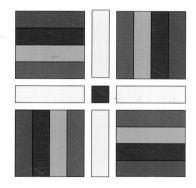

5 Sew the sashing between the two blocks in the top and bottom row. Press the seams towards the sashing.

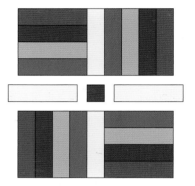

6 Sew the middle sashing strips together with a post in the middle. Press the seams towards the sashing strips.

7 Sew the three rows together and press the seams towards the sashing. Make nine of these blocks altogether.

8 Lay out the nine blocks in three rows of three, as shown on the facing page.

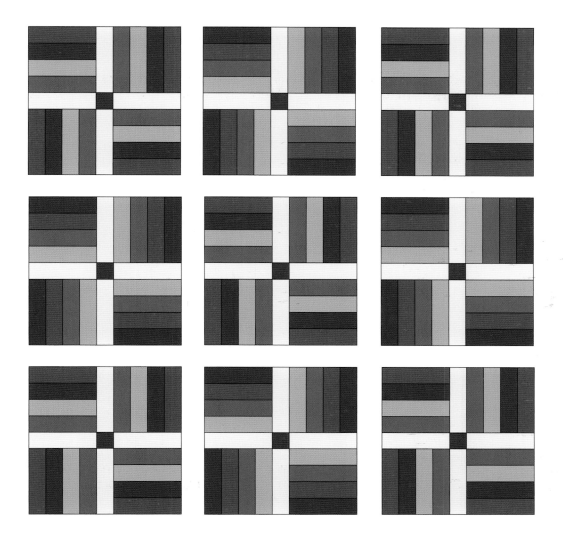

9 Sew the blocks in each row together, making sure you match up the sashing. Press the seams on each row in alternating directions.

10 Sew the three rows together, matching up the sashing as before. Press all the seams in one direction.

11 Cut four border strips each 54½in (138.5cm) long.

12 Sew two strips to opposite sides of the quilt. Press the seams towards the border.

13 Sew a corner square to each end of the remaining two border strips. Press the seams towards the border (see below).

14 Attach these to the quilt. Press the seams towards the border.

15 Layer and baste the patchwork top ready to be quilted (see pages 28–29).

16 Quilt using the Amish wave design, as I have, or any of the other quilting designs shown on pages 34–35.

17 When the quilting is complete, bind and label the quilt (see pages 36–40).

AUTUMN CUSHION

This matching cushion can be sewn from the extra block you made with the Autumn Floor quilt. It has a simple envelope opening on the back for inserting the pad, and is quick and easy to make.

1 Layer the block with the wadding and lining and baste them together. Use the Amish wave template (see pages 35 and 125) to mark the block and quilt it. Remove all the basting and trim the wadding and lining to the same size as the block. Square up the block if necessary.

2 On each piece of backing fabric, pin then stitch a double hem along one long side.

3 Lay the two pieces of backing fabric face down with the hemmed edges overlapping, forming a 20in (51cm) square. Lay the quilted block centrally on top, wrong sides facing, and pin it in place.

4 Make the binding and attach it to the top of the cushion, following the instructions on pages 37–38. The binding is sewn through the front of the cushion and the backing fabric, holding it all together.

5 Trim off the excess backing fabric.

6 Turn the binding over to the back of the cushion and finish attaching the binding by hand.

The completed cushion cover.

SWEET SIXTEEN

This simple 16-patch block makes the most of this pretty fabric collection. The country feel would make a charming addition to a young girl's bedroom, hence the name 'Sweet Sixteen'. I used a simple calico (muslin) as the alternating squares, but you could just as easily use a print for more texture.

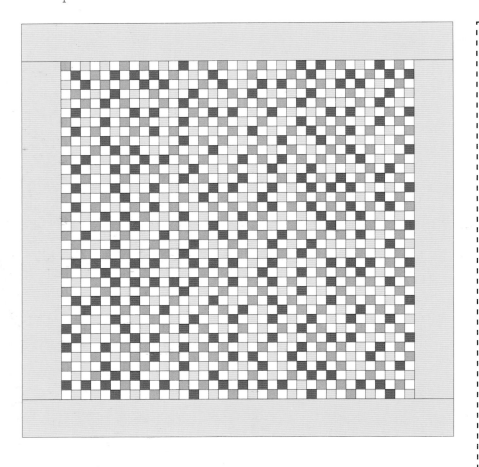

Measurements

Quilt size: 92 x 92in (233.5 x 233.5cm)
Block size: 8in (20.5cm) finished

Fabric requirements

One Jelly Roll™

For plain alternating squares: Cream Jelly Roll™ or 8¼ft (2.5m) of cream calico (muslin) cut into 40 strips each 2½in (6.5cm) wide.

Border: 6½ft (2m) Cut eight strips, 9½in (24cm) wide. Remove the selvedges and join to make a continuous length. Press the seams open.

Backing fabric: 23ft (7m) Cut into three equal lengths, remove selvedges and join. Press the seams open.

Wadding: 102 x 102in (259 x 259cm)

Binding: 27½in (70cm) Cut ten strips 2½in (6.5cm) wide.

METHOD

1 This method for sewing the block is very quick but still gives you a variety of fabrics in each block without repeats. Cut all of the 2½in (6.5cm) strips in half, so they all measure approximately 22in (56cm).

2 Pair up a print with a cream strip, right sides together, and machine stitch along the length. Press the seam towards the printed fabric.

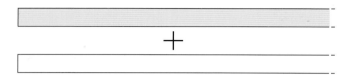

3 Trim off the selvedges. Cut the sewn strip into 2½in (6.5cm) segments. You should get about eight from each strip.

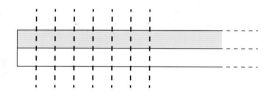

4 Repeat until all of the strips are sewn and cut.

5 Chain piece the segments together in pairs, in each case matching a square of printed fabric with a cream square. Press the seams towards the printed fabric. Mix up the prints and colours to avoid repetition.

6 Sew the rows of four squares together in pairs, alternating the printed squares with the cream squares. Because of the way you pressed the seams, they will lock together neatly.

7 Sew two of these pairs of rows together, again alternating the printed with the cream fabric, to create a 16-patch block.

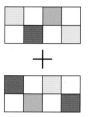

8 With a printed fabric square in the top left-hand corner, press all the seams in one direction.

9 Make 81 blocks for the quilt top altogether.

10 Lay out the quilt, nine blocks across and nine blocks down. Alternate the blocks according to the direction in which the seams are pressed.

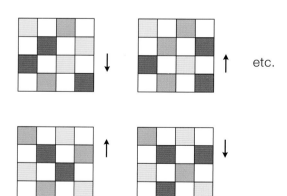

etc.

11 Sew the blocks together in rows. Again, because of the direction of pressing, the blocks will go together accurately and neatly.

12 Press the seams in each row in alternate directions.

13 Sew the rows together and press all the seams in one direction.

14 For the border, cut two pieces from the border strip each 72½in (184cm) long and sew them to opposite sides of the quilt. Press the seams towards the border.

15 Cut two strips each 90½in (230cm) long and sew them to the remaining two opposite sides. Press the seams towards the border.

16 Layer and baste the patchwork ready for quilting.

17 Choose one of the designs on pages 34–35 for the quilting.

18 Bind and label your quilt to finish (see pages 36–40).

NINE-PATCH BISCORNU

Beautifully embroidered biscornu have long been popular in
the embroidery world. They are pincushions sewn from two
offset squares that form an eight-sided shape. The French
word biscornu means odd, bizarre or irregular, but even
though the stitching method is somewhat unusual, this little
nine-patch biscornu makes a very pretty pincushion.

Measurements
6in (15cm) across, 2in
(5cm) high

Requirements
Nine 2½in (6.5cm) squares

Backing:
One piece of cotton velvet,
6½in (16.5cm) square

Filling:
Polyester toy stuffing or similar.
You could use birdcage grit
or bran as a filler as this helps
sharpen the pins and needles
as they are pushed into and
pulled out of the cushion, but
the biscornu may not keep its
shape as well.

Button, about 1¾in (4.5cm)
across

Strong thread for sewing on
the button, such as buttonhole
twist

1 Lay out the squares in three rows of three. Sew them together to make the nine-patch block. Press the seams.

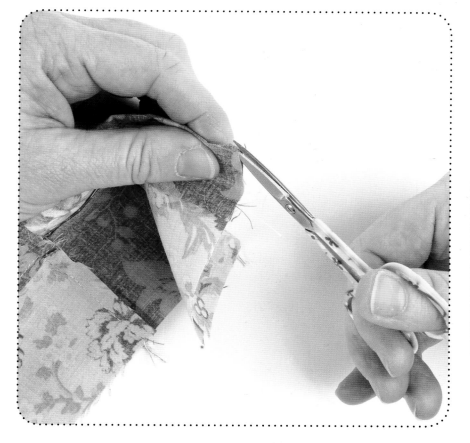

2 Mark the halfway point along each side of the block by folding it in half and snipping the fold with a sharp pair of scissors.

3 Mark the halfway point along each side of the backing fabric in the same way.

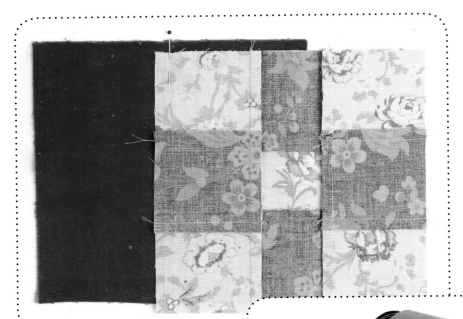

4 Place the two pieces of fabric right sides together, matching up the top left-hand corner of the block with the halfway point on the top edge of the velvet backing. Align the raw edges and pin the fabrics in place.

5 Stitch along the top of the block to the centre point, which should be aligned with the right-hand edge of the velvet.

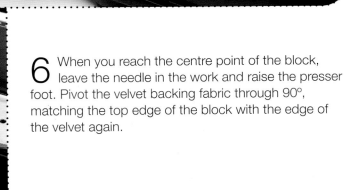

6 When you reach the centre point of the block, leave the needle in the work and raise the presser foot. Pivot the velvet backing fabric through 90°, matching the top edge of the block with the edge of the velvet again.

7 Continue to stitch until you reach the corner of the block, and pivot as before.

8 Continue to sew following this general rule: stitch until either the patchwork or the backing fabric runs out then pivot one fabric to align the raw edges and continue along. Stop when you reach the end of the seventh side.

9 Leave the last side unstitched and remove the shape from the machine.

The stitched shape.

10 Turn the shape the right way out and stuff firmly with the polyester toy stuffing. Slipstitch the opening closed using matching thread.

11 Thread a needle with a length of strong thread and make a knot in the end. Make a couple of stitches in the centre of the biscornu.

12 Attach the button, taking the needle through to the back of the pincushion with each stitch and pulling tightly on the thread to indent the biscornu.

The finished biscornu.

TEMPLATES

All of the templates shown on pages 124 to 126 are reproduced actual size. Simply copy them on to firm card or template plastic and cut neatly around the outline.

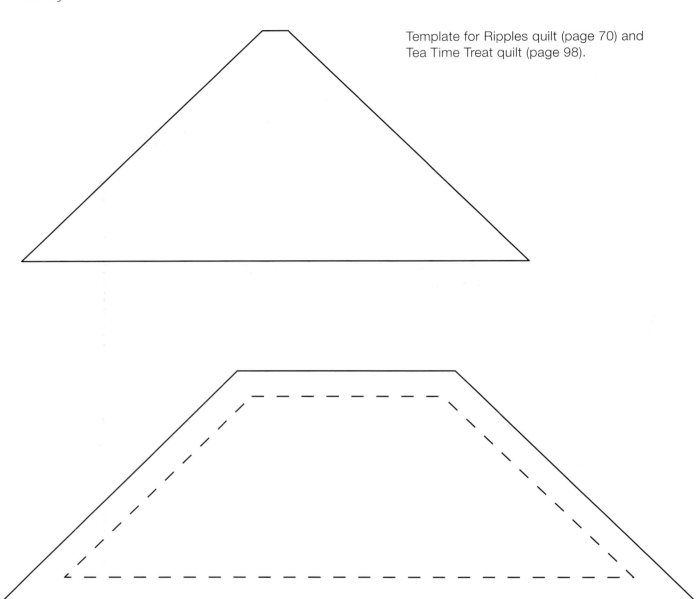

Template for Ripples quilt (page 70) and Tea Time Treat quilt (page 98).

Template for Sewing Spools quilt (page 80).

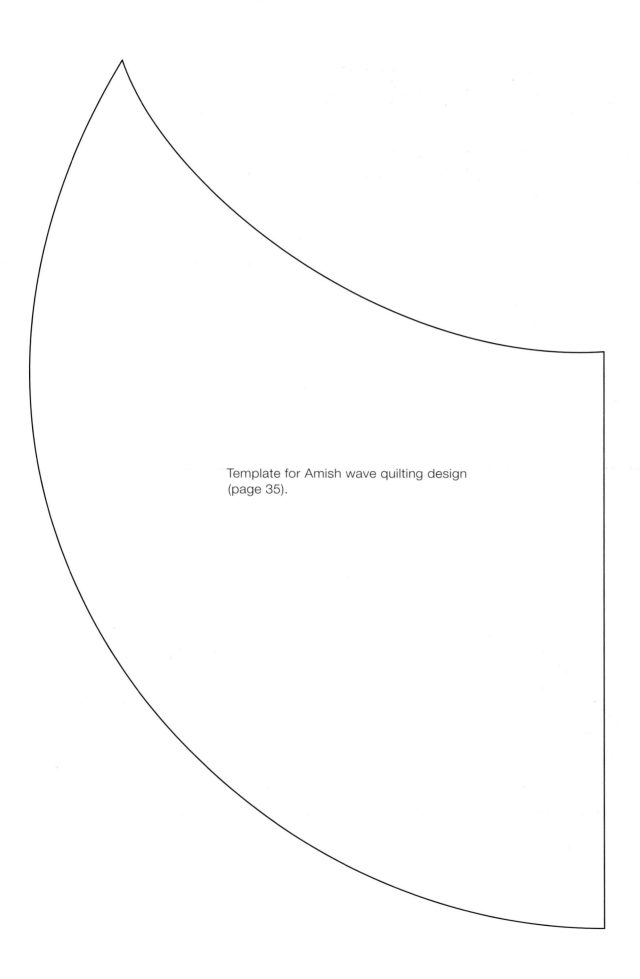

Template for Amish wave quilting design
(page 35).

Templates for Flower Garden quilt (page 52).

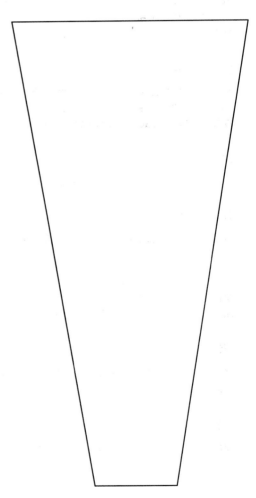

GLOSSARY

Binding

The fabric around the outside edge of the quilt that is applied when the quilting is finished to encase the raw edges.

Block

A design sewn from patchwork pieces that can be repeated to make a patchwork top. Blocks can be separated with sashing and posts.

Border

The fabric that surrounds the quilt around the outside of the patchwork.

Charm squares

Pre-cut fabric squares, usually 5 x 5in (13 x 13cm), that include samples from a particular fabric range. They are sold in packs of between forty and fifty squares.

Fat quarter

A fat quarter measures approximately 18 x 22in (50 x 56cm). It is a quarter of a square metre of fabric, obtained by cutting 18in (50cm) from the bolt of fabric and then cutting this in half to give a 'square'.

Frames

Strips of fabric that surround a patchwork block.

Patchwork

Pieces of fabric sewn together to form a design.

Post

A square of fabric or a block at the junction where the sashing strips meet, as on the Autumn Floor quilt, page 106.

Quilting

The running stitch or machine stitch that holds the three layers of a quilt together.

Sashing

Horizontal and vertical strips of fabric that go between the blocks of a quilt.

INDEX